D1472903

Great Cars From Chevrolet

BY THE EDITORS OF CONSUMER GUIDE®

CASTLE BOOKS

Contents

Louis Weber, President
Publications International, Ltd.
3841 West Oakton Street
Skokie, Illinois 60076

Permission is never granted for commerical purposes

This edition published by:
Castle Books
A Division of Book Sales, Inc.
110 Enterprise Avenue
Secaucus, N.J. 07094

Manufactured in the United States of America
1 2 3 4 5 6 7 8 9 10

Library of Congress Catalog Card Number: 80-81971
ISBN: 0-89009-346-6

Chief Contributing Author: Richard M. Langworth
Contributing Authors: Dick Larrowe, Ken Gross, Pat
Chappell, Michael Lamm

Photo Credits: Chevrolet Motor Division, GM Photographic,
David Gooley, Don Jensen, Michael Lamm, Richard M.
Langworth, Motor Vehicle Manufacturers Association, David
Newell, Pinky Randall, Bob Wingate

Cover Design: Frank E. Peiler

Portions of Chapters VI and VIII were excerpted from *The
Hot One: Chevrolet 1955–1957*, by Pat Chappell, courtesy of
Dragonwyck Publishing Inc., Contoocook, New Hampshire.
Portions of Chapters XIV and XV were excerpted from *The
Great Camaro*, by Michael Lamm, courtesy of Lamm-Morada
Publishing Company, Stockton, California. Chapter III was
originally published in *Special-Interest Autos*, Bennington,
Vermont.

Chevrolet: USA-1

Louis Chevrolet was the Andy Granatelli of his day, first racing cars, then designing them himself. His name came to prominence in 1905, when he raced successfully for Fiat's American branch in several contests including the Vanderbilt Cup, and beat the great Barney Oldfield on three occasions. Little did Chevrolet know that his name was destined to become a household word. Today, it stands for the best-selling automobile in the world—the most brilliant star in the General Motors constellation.

Chevrolet the man first came to the attention of GM founder William Crapo "Billy" Durant in 1907, who signed him and his brother Arthur as race drivers for Buick. (A third brother, Gaston, also raced with distinction.) But Durant lost control of GM soon after that, and left the corporation to regroup. Soon he was in charge of the Republic Motor Car Company of Hamilton, Ohio, and the Little Motor Company of Flint, Michigan. Durant then asked his friend Chevrolet to design a new car, and on November 3, 1911, founded a company to build it. Durant christened the car in Louis' honor, insuring immortality for Chevro-

let, and another tenure as head of General Motors for himself. Durant bought control of GM, largely with Chevrolet stock, in 1917, and folded in Chevy as the firm's new division.

Durant was forced out again in 1920, but the people who succeeded him, led by Alfred P. Sloan, built GM into the colossus it is today. Chevrolet had its ups and downs in the Teens and early '20s, but established itself as the company's chief weapon against Ford by 1923. Gradually, Chevy closed the sales gap between it and the legendary Model T by offering bigger, faster, brighter, and altogether superior cars for just a little more money. In 1927, when Henry Ford closed his factory to retool for the much-needed Model A, Chevrolet became the industry's top producer for the first time. Though Ford has had its moments in the half-century since, Chevrolet has continued to dominate the number-one spot in U.S. production. Today, Chevrolet would probably do quite well even if it were cut free from the vast General Motors empire. (Indeed, GM's enormous size and industry influence have led some to suggest this very thing.) It is questionable whether GM would do as well without Chevrolet.

In catering to as many buyers as possible, Chevy must please many tastes—and do so consistently year after year. Its success is shown by its perennially large market, which became increasingly diverse after World War II. The need to satisfy this market, not to mention its enormous financial resources, virtually guaranteed that Chevy would produce interesting and desirable cars of all kinds. It has—and that's what this book is all about.

Great cars from Chevy began coming off the lines almost from its beginnings, such as the winsome Baby Grand, the rakish Royal Mail, and the lovely Amesbury Special of the early Teens. Chevy pursued a one-model policy in the late Teens and '20s until Harley Earl arrived to set up the GM Art & Colour Studio in 1927. After that, a variety of deftly shaped body styles began to appear. The peaks of Chevy's pre-World War II design efforts were its 1932–33 models and the 1941 line. In both instances, GM Styling created some of the best-looking cars around—and there's a lot to read about them here.

Chevy's real diversification didn't come until after the war. It started with the 1949 redesign which, in one sweep, erased the prewar styles and replaced them with something dramatically different—stylish, low, and lovely. The year also witnessed the last of the genuine woody wagons, in which traditional construction was combined with the new styling to create one of the nicest cargo haulers ever made. For

Louis Chevrolet in one of his early racers

The first prototype Chevrolet, circa 1911

1950, Chevy added the rakish Bel Air hardtop. And for 1955, it skillfully fused the best elements of both wagon and hardtop design in the unforgettable Nomad.

The year 1955 was, of course, a milestone in Chevy's postwar story. That was the year that introduced freshly redesigned cars that have since become accepted as modern classics—not to mention an engine, the efficiently lively 265 V-8, that would foster a generation of Chevrolet high-performance machines. By 1957, this engine had grown to 283 cubic inches and, with the help of fuel injection, offered up to one horsepower per cubic inch. This was an unheard-of accomplishment for a mass-produced car, let alone one of the "low-priced three." But Chevrolet wasn't content with that. Diving right into another new market sector, it issued the luxurious Impala in 1958, the first of the smooth-riding, lavishly equipped Chevrolets exemplified by today's Monte Carlo and Caprice Classic.

The Corvette sports car, of course, is a story in itself, one treated by the editors in a separate book (see page 96). While everyone, it seems, has a favorite Corvette, the best (to our eyes) are the 1956–57 and 1963–67 generations—the most noteworthy in this distinguished line. The 1956 restyle made Corvette look like a serious sports car for the first time. The high-performance engines that followed in '57 made it one to be reckoned with on the race tracks of the world. The magnificent 1963 Sting Ray, which shone brilliantly but briefly through 1967, is probably the most timeless Corvette. With their larger V-8s, these cars were among the world's fastest and most beautiful two-seaters.

The Corvair is a car many people at Chevrolet would like to forget, if only its enthusiasts would let them. Born out of Edward N. Cole's revolutionary concepts, the Corvair was as different from conventional U.S. cars as a jet fighter is from a 747. For the first time, Americans could buy a popularly priced, mass-produced domestic car with four-wheel independent suspension, rear-mounted air-cooled engine, nimble handling, and a superb balance between performance and economy. Efficiency with reasonable size was the Corvair's long suit. It is ironic and regrettable that it died amidst a chorus of ill-advised charges made by well-meaning people who otherwise would have welcomed such a car. But the Corvair *did* last 10 years, and 1.7 million copies were built.

The Corvair Monza was the car that started the whole sporty car syndrome in America with its four-speed gearbox, luxurious bucket-seat interior, sprightly performance, and fun-to-drive nature. The turbocharged Monza Spyder and Corsa built on that basis, and many writers were not ashamed to label them poor man's Porsches. Indeed, they were.

Then there was the big, hairy Super Sport of 1961–63, with its 409 cubic-inch V-8 and at least that many horsepower, and its successor, the 1964–67 Impala SS—the fastest full-size cars Chevy ever built. And 1967 introduced the Camaro, which is with us yet—a handsome, roadable, high-performance automobile that is the essence of grand touring.

Together, these Chevys write an indelible record of innovation, performance, luxury, fine styling, and clever engineering. These are the cars that, if reasons are needed, helped make Chevy worthy of the title so often seen on showroom banners and courtesy plates: "USA-1." Chevrolet will probably always be USA-1 for many good reasons—starting with these 15 all-time greats.

William C. Durant

Alfred P. Sloan

Harley Earl

The Early Years:
Royal Mail
and Baby Grand

In July 1913, a small item in *The Automobile* announced the arrival in New York City of the Chevrolet Motor Company, led by one William Crapo Durant. The automotive world had already heard of Mr. Durant, and would hear more again: through this new venture, Durant would eventually regain control of General Motors. The public had heard much less of the Chevrolet car, though many knew of racing driver Louis Chevrolet. Yet, its reputation would grow quickly. Though it was no sales threat to Ford in those days, Chevrolet quickly launched some intriguing, well-built models that gained wide acceptance for the make.

Chevrolets built from early 1913 were all designated 1914 models. "Postdating" was common practice in the industry's early days, and has been seen more recently, too (as with the 1951 Kaiser and the 1965 Mustang). There were three types: the Series L (Light 6), the Series C, and the Series H. The Series L is notable in that it was the first Chevrolet to use the now-familiar "bow tie" emblem. Powered by a six-cylinder engine (the only flathead in the 1914 line), the L sold for $1475, complete with electric starter and light. The Series C was a luxury car, designed by the great Louis Chevrolet himself. It weighed 3500 pounds and was priced at $2500.

Preceding the bow-tie as Chevy's emblem was this script—Louis Chevrolet's signature.

But the Chevy that stood out most in those pioneer years was the four-cylinder Series H. Its overhead-valve engine, designed by Arthur Mason of the Mason Motor Company, was advanced for its time. It remained in use (with certain modifications) through 1928, and influenced the design of much later GM engines, such as the Opel Rekord four of the '50s, the Chevy II four of the '60s, and Pontiac's "Iron Duke" four of the late '70s. Originally, the bore and stroke of the Series H was 3.69×4.00, giving a displacement of 170.9 cubic inches and 21.38 rated horsepower. Splash lubrication, which would be a feature of Chevrolet powerplants through 1953, was typical for 1913, but would be a quaint curiosity 40 years later.

The Series H clutch was the cone type that would be used by Chevrolet for many years. Because it had a leather facing, the clutch was prone to grabbing if not properly anointed with leather softening oils. The transmission was located amidships on the end of a short shaft extending back from the engine. This, too, was a practice that endured into the '50s (in tractors), and the arrangement was used on many luxury cars in the Teens.

The Series H's rear axle was shaft-driven through bevel gears. A torque tube enclosed the driveshaft. Springs, bolted rigidly to the frame rails, were semi-elliptics up front and three-quarter elliptics in the rear. Ball-type wheel bearings were supplied to Chevrolet by the New Departure Company (also destined to become part of the GM empire), and were another feature retained by Chevy well into the '50s. They were often denigrated by critics as "bicycle bearings," but in fact gave good service when properly maintained.

Wheels were made of wood, but accessory wire types were available from several suppliers, most of whom also made wire wheels for Model T Fords. The Series H track was either 56 or 60 inches, depending on customer preference. The wider track, called the "Southern tread," was intended mainly for the Southern states where wagon tracks were of the

PINKY RANDALL

1914 Series H Royal Mail roadster (model H2)

same width. In those days, of course, most roads were dirt. To negotiate them after heavy rains, a car had to have a track wide enough to fit the inevitable ruts left behind by horse-drawn vehicles.

Without a doubt, the most memorable versions of the Series H Chevy were the Baby Grand touring and the Royal Mail roadster. Both were built at Chevrolet's factory in Flint, though a special touring car came from New York City. Prices were $875 for the Baby Grand and $750 for the Royal Mail. Standard equipment included Simms magneto with hand-crank starting. Electric lights and starter were optional at $125. Both cars shared the same chassis design, much as today's Impala and Caprice use the same chassis. Though both rode a 104-inch wheelbase, the Royal Mail was lighter than the Baby Grand. It carried 30×3.5-inch tires and weighed 1975 pounds, against 32×3.5-inch tires and 2200 pounds for the Baby Grand.

The Royal Mail, in particular, caught the fancy of early "car buffs," and perhaps endowed them with a

Walter Mittyish feeling of driving something more exotic than most other cars of the day. Its body, possibly on purpose, seemed to resemble nothing so much as the mighty Stutz. In performance, the Royal Mail was a far cry from the fabled Indianapolis-built machines, but it could out-accelerate a Model T Ford, and returned good gas mileage.

An early test of a Royal Mail occurred in September 1914, observed by "impartial automotive writer" J. E. Schipper. The place was New York City's Central Park. The car was a standard model taken from the showroom and equipped with a Stromberg Model K carburetor, the smallest available. The generator was disconnected, as was a connection between the brake and clutch pedals. Maintaining an average speed of 21.6 mph, the Royal Mail achieved 27.9 miles per gallon—a performance that might endear it today to the Department of Energy.

It should be noted that 20 mph was about as fast as anyone could drive in those years (the Lincoln Highway was still mainly a dream in the minds of a few in-

7

1913 Series H Baby Grand touring (model H4)

dustrialists). The Chevrolet owner's manual noted that 40 mph was "excessive speed," so the slow pace of that Royal Mail test car was probably more practical than it appears today. The car was certainly flexible. During the outing, it climbed an 8-percent grade in direct drive at 16 mph, without ping, on 70-octane gasoline, while pulling a 4:1 axle ratio.

Most 1914 Chevrolets came from the Flint factories, and sales prospects convinced Durant to predict a run of 8500 cars. Actually, about 5000 were sold, including an estimated 2500 Royal Mails. The pretty roadsters came with "Chevrolet gray" body and wheels and had black-painted chassis. Green and plum were also available and it was common for dealers to offer other colors to suit customers. Gray was much too drab.

Early in the 1914 model run, a styling change took place in the Series H line. The flat wooden dash was replaced by a more streamlined hood and cowl. This led many owners of earlier versions to believe that their cars were '13s—closer to the truth than some might admit, though it doesn't agree with Chevrolet's official dating policy.

The success of the Series H forced other Chevrolet models out of production. The "C" disappeared during 1913 and the "L" vanished during 1915, though leftovers may have been in the showrooms for a year or so afterward. Meanwhile, the Series H line was expanded with the 1915 addition of the H3 Amesbury Special. A "top-of-the-line" Royal Mail, this model featured more modern styling, which again exhibited a marked similarity to that of Stutz. In place of the exposed oval fuel tank behind the seat, as seen on the first- and second-generation Royal Mails, the H3 had a flat decklid that hid the tank. It also sported wire wheels and a canvas wind deflector mounted behind the driver. One throwback, however, was its older cowl design, the wooden dashboard or firewall as used on the early 1914 models. The rest of the 1915 line retained the streamlined cowl previously mentioned.

The Amesbury Special came only in French gray, a sort of off-white. The most common contemporary photo of this car shows actress Bonita Sterling at the wheel. Not much is known about Bonita, but in 1915 she may have been as famous as Bo Derek is today. The car, too, is not well-known, though a few examples have survived and have been restored. Amesbury Specials were available only for 1915.

The Amesbury, the "basic" Royal Mail, and the Baby Grand all shared a 106-inch wheelbase in 1915, and all had larger-diameter brakes—12 instead of 10 inches. The engine, which by then was referred to as "valve-in-head," was attracting considerable attention and praise. As one magazine put it, "The head is a one-piece casting secured to the cylinder block by bolts, the joint being made with a copper and asbestos gasket." Reporters marveled over the fact that the head contained the valves, valve springs, and rocker arms, topped by a nickel-plated valve cover. Pushrods extended up from cam followers, operating rocker arms that opened and

1914 Series H Royal Mail roadster (model H2)

1915 Series H Royal Mail roadster (model H2)

1915 Series H Amesbury Special (model H3)

closed the valves. Valves and valve stems were cooled by a water jacket in the head. These features may seem unremarkable today; in 1915, with the flathead engine nearly universal, they were considered sensational. It wasn't until 1955 that Chevrolet stopped referring to its ohv engines as "valve-in-head"— the slogan wore that well.

If a Royal Mail was ordered without electric lights and starter, it came with a Simms magneto. If ordered with electric lights, the system provided was made by Auto Lite, with a Connecticut Electric distributor/coil instead of a magneto. The 1915 starter was located at the rear of the engine, operating a ring gear on the flywheel as in a modern car, rather than at the front of the engine as in the 1914 Series H. The cooling system remained, as it had been, a thermo syphon without water pump. While Royal Mails used a gravity-flow fuel tank, the 1915 Baby Grand featured a Steward-Warner vacuum tank.

An estimated 500 Amesbury Specials and 2500 Royal Mails were built for 1915. Overall, Chevrolet turned out 13,000 cars that year, and entered the top ten in production for the first time in its history.

There were no major changes in the Chevy line for 1916, though the Amesbury Special was discontinued. An open driveshaft appeared on New York–built cars. An ammeter was now included in the base price of $750, along with the previously extra-cost electric starter, lights, distributor, generator, and six-volt Willard battery.

Though the older H2 Royal Mail remained in production, it was joined that year by the sharp-looking H2½. This had green wheels and body, a black chassis and fenders, and a cellular (instead of tubular) radiator. About 16,000 of the 1916 Series H cars were made altogether. There is no precise production breakdown by model, but estimates would suggest about 8000 Royal Mail roadsters of both styles. These pretty little open Chevys were no longer in the limelight, however, for 1916 had seen the birth of the 490 (named for its $490 base price), which sent sales soaring. Total production for the year, at 62,898, put Chevy into seventh place in the industry, hard on the heels of Studebaker. For 1917, Chevrolet would run fourth behind Ford, Willys-Overland, and Buick.

By 1917, World War I was preoccupying the nation's economy. But car production didn't stop completely, as in World War II; rather, it leveled off as the auto industry turned to defense work, as it would in the Korean conflict. Chevrolet, however, continued to grow, and in 1918 became part of General Motors. W. C. Durant then regained control of GM by trading his valuable Chevrolet stock for GM stock. In fact, Chevrolet acquired GM, rather than the other way round.

But Durant's second period at the helm was not marked by great accomplishment. By nature a speculator, Durant was most happy engineering complicated acquisitions or mergers, and perhaps paid less attention than he should have to the firm's day-to-day affairs. He also tried to support GM shares on the stock market through personal investment. When the market slumped in September 1920, Durant was faced with financial catastrophe. Pierre S. duPont, whose much greater fortune had also been brought to bear to save faltering GM, ultimately took over from Durant as president in November 1920. But by then, the real administrative authority was being wielded by Alfred P. Sloan, a dynamic young executive who would go on to become GM's president— and, most agree, its greatest.

During Durant's presidency, Chevrolet relied chiefly on the 490, and gradually discontinued its larger cars. The Royal Mail and Baby Grand shown in 1917 sales literature were listed as part of a new Model F series, and were considerably different from their Series H predecessors. Both were continued right on through 1922, though the model names were deleted after 1917. Chevrolet had no doubt observed that later versions bore little resemblance to the originals.

The 1917 Model F Royal Mail had a body similar to the 490's with a 108-inch wheelbase. Price was $800. In later years, wheelbase was lengthened to 110 inches. For 1918, engine capacity was increased to 224 cid and a water pump was fitted. Though they were good performers, the Model Fs lacked much of the character that makes the earlier Royal Mail and Baby Grand so noteworthy today. Chevrolet was entering a new age.

Chevys from the Golden Age: 1932 and 1933

According to the ledgers, 1932–33 was a terrible period for Chevrolet. The division had wrested first place from Ford in 1931 with over 600,000 cars for the calendar year, and held that position in 1932–33. But in the depths of the Depression, volume was cut in half. Chevy's total for calendar 1932 was just 306,716 cars; in 1933 it was 481,134. The division hadn't seen such low volume since 1924.

Nevertheless, Chevrolet enthusiasts tend to wax ecstatic over the 1932–33 models, and the reason is not hard to understand. These were the most strikingly beautiful Chevys since the Royal Mail, and possibly the most beautiful ever.

The 1932–33 period represented a transition. Styling began to move away from the four-square upright shapes of the 1920s toward more aerodynamic forms, a trend that culminated in the 1934 Chrysler Airflow and the 1936 Lincoln-Zephyr. For many makes, including Chevrolet, the styling of the early '30s was an ideal compromise—just the right combination of classic and streamlined design. As a reason for the Model A Ford's popularity, collectors often cite its resemblance to the larger, more luxurious Lincoln. In the same way, the 1932–33 Chevys resembled the 1932–33 Cadillacs—and those were among the most beautiful Cadillacs of all time.

Another advantage of these Chevys, from the collector's standpoint, is that many of them were "loaded." In those deep Depression years, more and more Chevy buyers came from the upper-income bracket—people who, in better times, would have purchased larger cars, or who had the money but didn't want to flaunt it. Chevrolet recognized this, and aimed a series of magazine advertisements at its new-found clientele. Thus, 1932–33 models tended to be fitted with more options than were normally common for a low-priced make. A wealthy individual could avoid the resentment of less-fortunate fellows by buying a fully-equipped, top-of-the-line Chevrolet instead of, say, a plain Buick. In many cases, the loaded Chevrolet actually cost more. The happy result, many generations later, is that surviving 1932–33 models tend to be well-equipped, and many of them are open body styles.

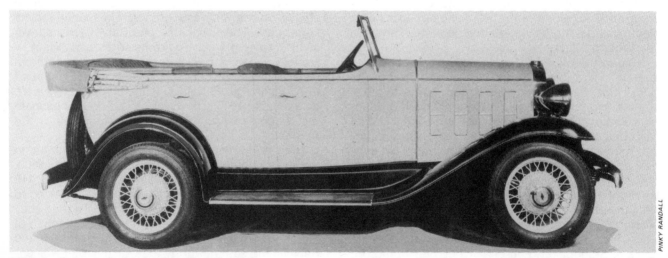

1932 Confederate Series BA Standard phaeton

1932 Confederate Series BA DeLuxe sports roadster

The 1932 Chevrolet was designated Series BA "Confederate," a curious name that was used only this one year. In those days, Chevrolet used supplemental names to denote each model year. Previous entries included "International," "Independence," and "Universal."

Mounted on a 109-inch-wheelbase chassis was Chevy's inline six, displacing 194 cubic inches (bore and stroke 3.31 × 3.75). It provided 60 bhp at 3000 rpm, and drove through a 4.10:1 rear axle ratio. The engine, descended from designs dating back to the Royal Mail, featured 20 percent more horsepower, a stiffer crankcase, and a heavier counterbalanced crankshaft compared to the 1931 version. Its smoothness was enhanced with rubber mounts located in

"Diamond" fashion at the front of the engine, on the sides of the clutch housing, and at the rear of the transmission. This arrangement was used by Chevrolet through 1951. The small clutch housing mounts tended to give trouble but, when installed with shims to prevent stretching, were usually reliable. The engine also featured a quiet four-blade fan, replacing the earlier two-blade fan. Halfway through the model year, the transmission gears became helical-cut instead of straight-cut, providing what Chevrolet duly called "Silent Second." Finally, there was a downdraft carburetor, hood ventilator doors instead of louvers, a cowl vent, and 18-inch road wheels. The transmission was a synchromesh type, based on the Cadillac design introduced in 1928.

All these changes were aimed at greater driving ease and passenger comfort, and were clearly intended to one-up the competition, namely Dearborn and Highland Park. A 1932 Chevy slogan was "Six Cylinders—No More, No Less." As the company was careful to explain, "With more you sacrifice economy—with less, you sacrifice smoothness." So much, in Chevy's opinion, for the Ford V-8 and the Plymouth four.

Following the lead of the 1930 Studebaker, Chevrolet went to free-wheeling for its '32 models. This mechanical device was designed to allow the clutch driving member to impart motion to its driven member in only one direction. Plymouth also featured it, but while free-wheeling appeared on Lincolns, it was never seen on Fords. Chevrolet's unit was supplied by the L.G.S. Manufacturing Company, which built similar ones for Auburn and Duesenberg.

The free-wheeling mechanism consisted of front

1932 Confederate Series BA phaeton (Holden body)

11

1932 Confederate Series BA Standard roadster (trunk model)

and rear cups with a coil spring between them, mounted at the rear of the transmission. As power was applied, the spring expanded into the cups to move the car. With power off, the spring slipped, releasing the cups, which were then free to rotate. The unit could be locked out by a dashboard control.

Chevrolet's owner manual stated that free-wheeling "permits the car to glide freely and quietly with the engine turning at idling speed, although the transmission is in gear and the clutch engaged. When free-wheeling is in operation, the engine drives the car in the usual way to the desired speed; then by releasing the accelerator, the engine returns to idling speed, while the car wheels on easily since it is not required to drive the engine at an equivalent speed. Free-wheeling is operative on all speeds except reverse."

Ostensibly, the main benefits of free-wheeling

1932 Confederate Series BA landau phaeton (shown at the New York Auto Show)

1932 Confederate Series BA DeLuxe phaeton

were enhanced fuel economy and less engine wear. But there was a drawback: without engine braking available in free-wheeling, a considerable extra strain was placed on the brakes. Chevrolet's four-wheel brakes were mechanical and as good as anybody's, but mechanical brakes were just not as effective as hydraulics. And although the owner's manual warned against the use of free-wheeling on hills, inexperienced drivers all too often forgot to use the lockout, resulting in hair-raising downhill rides. On some occasions, the lockout actually broke—at the worst possible moment. Free-wheeling quickly gained a dubious reputation, was banned in several states, and vanished among American cars almost as quickly as it appeared.

Inside the 1932 Chevrolet was evidence of attention to detail and convenience. The fuel gauge was a new type utilizing a single cork float in the tank, which had a baffle plate to prevent surging. A sending unit was connected to the gauge, mounted in front of the driver on the instrument panel. All wires and cables to the engine compartment were routed through a rubber block mounted on the firewall—a feature Chevrolet would retain for many years. The front seat was adjustable on all models except the roadster and phaeton. Two heavy hinges were used on each door instead of the previous three light hinges, except on the cabriolet and landau.

Visibility was better in 1932 than it had been before, largely because of the body design. The front fenders had deep crowns and skirts with wide beads at the edges; the rear fenders had crowns and long, tapering ends. Headlights were deeper, but smaller in diameter and fitted with convex lenses. Chrome-plated, Klaxon-built, trumpet-type horns were used in lieu of the flat "pancake" horns of 1931. One horn

was standard, a second was optional. Reflector-type glass lenses were used for headlights and cowl lamps, and convex lenses covered the instrument dials. The windshield wiper motor was located inside the car, and a carpeted kickpad was added to the phaeton's rear compartment. Ashtrays were standard equipment (except on the roadster and phaeton).

The Confederate series for 1932 included a roadster, phaeton, sport roadster, landau phaeton, coach, cabriolet, three-window coupe, five-window coupe, sedan, sport coupe, and special sedan. The roadster was the lightest at 2515 pounds, with the rest of the line ranging between this and the special sedan's 2845 pounds.

In preparation for what appeared to be a splendid new product, Chevrolet put its factories back on a five-day work week. Its some 36,000 employees now averaged 50 man-hours per week, as opposed to 32 the previous winter. In March 1932, Chevrolet reported an 81 percent gain in fleet sales compared to 1931. In April, Chevy and GM's other products were shown amidst green-and-gold cloth-draped backdrops in 55 American cities. The exhibit slogan was "Work for Many Hands." President Hoover, in a pep talk designed to aid industry sales, called buying a new car "a badge of honor" because it kept people working. But sales were generally a disappointment compared to previous years.

The long-awaited Ford V-8 appeared in March 1932, and Chevrolet immediately cut prices to meet the challenge. The roadster now cost only $445, while a Ford V-8 roadster sold for $460—and $15 seemed like much more then than it does now. But other Ford and Chevrolet models were priced almost identically. Chevrolet, however, announced it had no intention of building anything except six-cylinder cars for the immediate future—and faithfully kept its word until 1955.

Though upper-class customers proved helpful to Chevrolet in 1932, the make's traditional low- and middle-income buyers were scarce indeed. Generally, small cars like Chevy lost some 50 percent of their 1931 volume. But Chevy's situation that year was hardly helped by the competition. Aside from the new Ford, there was the attractive, economical Plymouth with ads that begged the public to "Look at All Three." There was also Hudson's new Essex Terraplane priced about $20 lower than comparable Chevys. (Chevrolet countered this by dropping base price by $18.) Some medium-priced cars were less affected by the sales slump; Dodge actually moved into third place. But for the "low-priced three," 1932 was a disappointing year. At Chevrolet, there was a decline in employment to only 18,610 workers by November, when the changeover to the 1933 line began.

The new models received a complete body change, and again looked like scaled-down versions of then-current Cadillacs. Sales were up by better than 50 percent for the calendar year, and the model year figure was around 600,000.

1933 Eagle (Master) Series CA phaeton

The 1933 line, covering a price spread between $485 and $580, carried the model designation "Eagle." This term was replaced by "Master" by the end of 1933, though the eagle hood mascot featured that year was present in one form or another through 1956. A second line of less-expensive closed two-doors was introduced in March 1933 as the Mercury series. Like Eagle, this name was dropped after just one year (only to return on the medium-priced car launched for 1938 by Chevy's arch rival in Dearborn). Successor to the Mercury was the Chevrolet Standard. The 1933 Mercury was mainly intended for fleet markets, and its engine parts were not interchangeable with the Eagle's. Destroked from 1932, the Mercury six displaced 180.9 cubic inches (3.31 × 3.50), and produced 60 bhp at 3000 rpm.

The Eagle was the line that carried on the elegant tradition of the 1932 Confederate. For it, Chevrolet engineers enlarged their six-cyclinder power unit to 206.8 cubic inches (3.31 × 4.00) for an output of 65 bhp at 2800 rpm. Featured were automatic spark control with centrifugal weights and vacuum advance, a cooling system thermostat, and a 14-gallon fuel tank. Accessories included a six-tube "superheterodyne"

1933 Eagle (Master) Series CA sport coupe

radio, a choice of leatherette or metal tire covers, defroster, cigar lighter, license plate frame, Eagle mascot, rearview mirror glare shield, and spring covers. Free-wheeling was carried over from 1932 for Eagle models only. A new piece of standard equipment was the "Starterator." This automatic starter had a vacuum unit that engaged the starter motor to the accelerator pedal when there was no engine vacuum. When the engine caught, the vacuum disengaged the starter linkage.

The 1933 frame was a double-drop affair that lowered overall height by about three inches at the cowl. The opening windshield of 1932 was fixed on closed cars, which now featured Fisher's "No-Draft" ventilation system with small pivoting wing vents at the forward corners of the side windows. "No-Drafts" remained a Chevrolet feature through 1967, and many found their 1968 replacement, a forced-air flow-through system, inadequate by comparison.

By some standards, 1933 could be called a year of gadgets. The cars featured an air-bleed device that prevented throttle engagement at high engine speeds. There was also an "Octane Selector" on the side of the distributor to compensate for the quality of fuel being used.

The rear axle was redesigned for 1933 with the wheels bolted directly to flanges on the ends of the axle shafts. The axle was removed by pulling out washers at the inside ends. Separate parking brake shoes were eliminated, and service brakes were connected to the handbrake lever. A large muffler was used to reduce back pressure, and was mounted on a small leaf spring to allow it to move with the engine.

The 1933 models had an unusual riveted universal joint designed so that the only way to change the joint was to remove the differential housing. Many owners simply chiseled it out and eliminated the rivets by bolting the device together. This avoided the necessity of pulling the rear end every time a universal needed work or a clutch required replacement.

The variety of open styles, offered only in the Eagle series, was reduced considerably from 1932. There were only three of them: the sports roadster (2867 built), the convertible cabriolet (4276 built), and the phaeton (543 built). All sold new for under $600, even when equipped with every accessory in the book. Many of these more expensive Chevys sported the faddish new 9.00×13-inch "donut" tires—built especially for Ford and Chevrolet, which offered special wheels to mount them on. One brand was General's "Jumbo." The donuts passed away during the early '30s, but they were not unlike the modern tires used for off-road vehicles today.

Chevrolet was no doubt loath to dwell on the performance of its '33 cars, especially after the low-priced Mercury appeared in March. It turned out to be faster than the Eagle. The Mercury used a 107-inch wheelbase against the Eagle's 110, and was lighter by some 400 pounds. The weight difference was too much for the Eagle's larger engine to over-

1933 Eagle (Master) Series CA DeLuxe sports roadster

come. A Mercury owner could also build his own high-performance car quite easily by simply bolting in an Eagle engine. Quite a few did so. Of course, the factory never built them that way.

Because of nicer styling and the wider variety of sporty open models offered, the '32 Chevy has more appeal than the '33 among today's connoisseurs of the marque. This means more '32s have been found and restored—roughly four times as many compared to the '33 model. Don Jensen of the Vintage Chevrolet Club of America has compiled the following estimates of survivors:

Body style	Production	Survivors
phaeton	419	20
roadster (trunk model)	1118	80
sport roadster (rumble seat)	8552	75
cabriolet	7066	65
landau phaeton	1602	25

What are they worth today? That question defies hard and fast figures. Prices vary greatly depending on the car's condition, the readiness of the owner to sell, and the eagerness of the buyer. Chevrolet club sources have estimated that a perfectly restored phaeton could be worth from $25,000 to $30,000 today, which seems reasonable. Roadsters or cabriolets would sell for $5000 to $7000 less. Landau phaetons are estimated to fall in the $20,000–$25,000 range.

But bear in mind that this applies only to "100-point" authentic restorations. You can still get into a 1932–33 Chevy for under five figures, and take your time on a restoration. In the opinion of many collectors, the project would be well worth the expense, time, and trouble. To those with a broad understanding of cars, these are the true "classic Chevys." While not "pedigreed" Classics like Duesenbergs or Packards, they nevertheless set some of the highest standards of design, performance, and engineering for the low-priced field in the '30s.

15

1941: The Definitive Chevy

Although 1941 Chevys are no longer such a common sight, there was a time when it seemed almost everybody had one—or at least had driven one. It may not have been an exciting car, but it *was* practically universal—as hardy and persistent as a dandelion, as smooth and appealing as homemade vanilla ice cream.

In the autumn of 1940, Americans were increasingly aware of the war raging in Europe. Though the storm clouds overseas hadn't affected automobile production at home, buyers seemed to anticipate the coming conflict. Many looked carefully at the new 1941 models with an eye to how long these cars might have to last.

Cars were already becoming lower, longer, and wider in the early '40s, and the '41 Chevy—destined to continue into the postwar world through 1948—was no exception. It certainly had the right formula. Chevy romped home ahead of Ford in 1941, with record sales of cars and trucks for the sixth straight year. At 930,293, calendar year car output was the third highest in history, trailing only the banner pre-Depression years of 1927 and 1929.

Chevrolet engineers and designers were careful not to do anything too radical with the '41 because

the 1940 model had been a complete departure for Chevy's evolutionary styling policy. But although it was only a facelift of a one-year-old theme, the '41 model is much better remembered by enthusiasts today. It is the definitive Chevy.

Ken Coppock was in charge of the Chevrolet styling studio when the 1941 models took shape. Coppock had begun his career as a painter and striper; he was then apprenticed as a designer at the Locke Body Company in Rochester, New York. There Coppock trained under the sure hand of John Tjaarda, who would win fame in the '30s as the gifted creator of the Lincoln-Zephyr.

When Locke folded after the 1929 Wall Street crash, Coppock did full-scale drafting at LeBaron, then part of the Briggs Manufacturing Company. At LeBaron, he again worked with Tjaarda and with Ralph Roberts. "But when the opportunity came up at GM in 1932, I went with them and stayed until I retired," Coppock recalled. "I started as a draftsman, was an engineering advisor in the Chevrolet studio, then became a designer, and finally was promoted to head up the studio. At the time, we worked in little cubicles on one floor in the GM Building. In 1937, we moved to separate studios.

"Harley Earl took an active part in all our designs," Coppock continued, referring to the legendary head of the Art & Colour Studio, and father of styling at General Motors. "His system was mainly to let each studio come up with its own ideas and sketches. Then he'd sit down and go over them as a critic. He'd ask questions, and finally he'd use the ideas from the studio as well as his own. He'd pick out one or two concepts worth exploring and we'd proceed from there. Earl . . . was one of the finest critics of design that ever came along.

"Mr. Earl would frequently come into Chevrolet with ideas from the other studios. We never knew that exactly, but I always suspected that was his technique. He'd sort of play one studio against the other. He was very good at that, too. 'Oh boy,' he'd say, 'they've got a design over in the Pontiac studios that's a good one. You guys aren't coming up with 'em like they are.'

"Of course, that sort of inspirational talk would have us all trying to beat Pontiac. I think Harley also

1941 Special DeLuxe four-door in the great outdoors

Spencer Tracy (left) admiring his '41 woody
with assistant sales manager W. G. Lewellen

liked to pick up an idea from one studio and take it into another and say, 'Why don't we try it this way?' And, of course, it was something he'd just seen next door.

"Chevrolet in 1939 looked like a scaled-down Cadillac—and that was Earl's idea, too. He wanted us to make Chevrolet similar to Cadillac, not a carbon copy, of course. People who couldn't afford a Cadillac were very satisfied with Chevrolet. The strategy worked for awhile and then we started making the car look like a Buick."

It is interesting to compare Coppock's remarks on the '39 Chevrolet with the styling directives applied to the classic 1932–33 models. Evidently, GM's master stylist never changed his design philosophy, for the earlier cars were overtly Cadillac-influenced. The Buick look, which came to the fore in 1940–41, was partly due to the work of a young stylist named Ned Nickles. Fittingly, Nickles would later graduate to head the Buick studio, where he was responsible for that make's trademark portholes and sweepspear treatment of the late '40s and beyond.

"Ned was one of those guys with cars coming out of his ears," recalled Coppock. "He was quite gifted." Nickles himself said that the effort to model the Chevrolet after the Buick was "a conscious thing. They both had overhead-valve engines and other similar characteristics, like torque-tube drive."

Former GM stylist George A. Jergenson also confirmed that the Chevrolet-Buick styling resemblance was intentional: "For 1940, like all GM's cars, Chevrolet's headlights came down off the grille and went into the fenders. We wanted a longer light [opening] than we'd had on the side of the hood, to make it more streamlined. So we decided to model it after Buick, splitting the light in half to make it longer . . . In 1936, I had worked with Frank Hershey on the Opel Kapitän [in Germany]. We had lights in the fenders and then ran the fenders right back into the doors. But we couldn't afford to do that in Detroit, so Chevrolet had to wait until 1941 for headlamps fully integrated into the fenders, and for 1942 for the fadeaway [fender] treatment."

More frequently, GM managers allowed Chevrolet to do whatever it wanted because of its high volume. Designer and body engineer Vince Kaptur, Sr. remembered: "Chevrolet wanted their own body—before the birth of the B-O-P body concept—and they weren't anxious to share body designs. After all, their production was in the millions. They could easily pay for designs, tools, and dies themselves. The other divisions with smaller production had to share and, of course, compromise. That's why GM instituted the interchangeability idea with die inserts and things of that nature—so they could get a different appearance as far as trim was concerned in moldings, window reveals, and other components."

Ned Nickles worked on the '42 Chevrolet but owned a '41. "I personally feel that when Chevrolet left the '39 model and came into 1940, they were in a big change . . . the '41 looked heavier and bigger. You got out of the Chevrolet size—the new model was more important-looking. The body sections were larger and more powerful."

1941 Special DeLuxe cabriolet (convertible)

Strother MacMinn of the Art Center College of Design in Pasadena, California, is another GM styling veteran. Although he didn't work on the '41 Chevrolet, his description of the car makes a rather prosaic-appearing design sound almost spiritual: "The

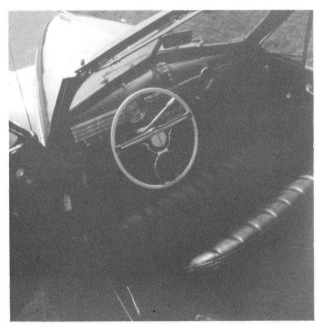

The 1941 Chevrolet dashboard

1940–41, with a stamped, squared-up version of Paul Browne's cloverleaf 1939 Buick grille, was a radical departure from the '39 Chevy. The shape of the hood was bolder—in keeping with the trend Harley Earl had adopted with Cadillac. They were getting away from the influence of the Lincoln-Zephyr's sharp prow front. Instead, Chevrolet used a horizontal-bar grille that would wrap around the nose of the hood and then curve smoothly into the fenders.

"The filleted catwalk was an important part of the development of the grille. Stylists were attempting to get to horizontal grille shapes despite the engineers' emphasis on vertical radiator cores. The theory at the time was to have as much direct airflow to the core as possible—the side openings were thought of as additional; they didn't count.

"The bold bars on the '41's grille are noteworthy. They had little bevels that caught the light and added to the viewing interest. The three red lines in the grille were definitely Harley Earl's idea—to add brightness and light value. The side molding also had a red-painted insert. [Stylists] would fight for black lines occasionally, because they'd accent comfortably with any body color, but Earl insisted on red.

"Chevrolet . . . wanted that kind of strong, bold statement. The red lines were all part of helping Chevrolet to identify itself. There seemed to be an alliance of corporate sensitivity, that Harley Earl was governing, that supplied the basic form for Chevrolet."

To many eyes, the '41 Chevrolet presents a more streamlined appearance than its 1940 predecessor, accentuated by a lower belt molding and headlamps integrated directly into the fenders. The long, rather graceful front fender ornamentation underscored fleetness in the idiom of the day. Streamlining was further supported by the sharply angled windshield raked at 49 degrees, versus 53 degrees in 1940. The coupe's backlight was also very rakish at 45 degrees, versus 51 degrees for the previous year.

Styling aside, Chevy was greatly improved for 1941, though in an evolutionary way. Two series were offered: the Special DeLuxe and its less expensive companion, the Master DeLuxe. Special DeLuxe equipment included more luxurious trim, illuminated clock, two-spoke steering wheel, stainless steel mouldings, front armrests, automatic domelight switch, ash "receiver," and carpeted inserts in the floormats. Convertibles and station wagons were offered only in Special trim.

Both series now shared Chevrolet's A-arm independent front suspension, which buyers had been opting for six to one. They also seemed to want larger cars, so the wheelbase on the '41 was stretched three inches to 116, and overall width was nearly two inches greater. All this translated into more usable interior space. With flared doors extending out over concealed running boards, the floor width between the bodysides was about four inches more than in 1940, though roof width remained the same. Front seat passengers gained about three inches more hiproom.

Under the hood, Chevy's four-main-bearing, 216.5-cid six (introduced in 1937) featured detail improvements and a new cylinder head. Advertising proclaimed a boost from 85 to 90 bhp ". . . for even greater gas and oil economy in addition to the lightning acceleration for which Chevrolet cars are famous." This was a pretty direct swipe at the 85-bhp Ford V-8, which was bested in power by Ford's own flathead six introduced in mid-1941. (After introducing the 90-bhp six, Ford cagily increased the V-8's power rating to 90.)

The 1941 Chevy's extra horsepower came from slightly increased compression (up to 6.5:1 from 6.25:1) plus redesigned combustion chambers and pistons. Engineers lowered the roof around the intake valves, and the domed slugs of the "Stovebolt Six" gave way to flat tops. Like Buick and Packard, Chevy made the mistake of converting from 14mm to 10mm spark plugs this year. It later went back to the original size.

A recurring Chevy problem, excess oil reaching intake valve stems, was virtually eliminated this year by capping the cup-like valve seats with umbrella-shaped metal covers. Water jacketing around the exhaust valve seats was increased, and a second water outlet aided cooling. The number of radiator fins was upped from four to five per inch. A sponge-rubber seal between the top of the radiator core and the hood prevented air leakage. The twin horns were moved out of the airstream and positioned sideways to keep them from being clogged with snow or slush.

A new higher-voltage, oil-filled coil was mated with a 50-percent greater-capacity condenser. Steeper lobes on the breaker cam separated the points more rapidly, and reduced arcing and pitting. Another point protector—interesting but virtually unknown—took the form of a rotary switch that reversed the flow of primary current whenever the starter pedal was depressed.

Other mechanical improvements included a re-

Special De Luxe
CABRIOLET

1941 Special DeLuxe cabriolet (convertible)

1941 Special DeLuxe station wagon

1941 Special DeLuxe Town Sedan

1941 Master DeLuxe Sport Sedan

1941 Special DeLuxe Sport Sedan

worked 1.5-inch Carter carburetor, with a lowered idle tube orifice to prevent stalling. The 1941 Chevy also received larger wheel spindles, strengthened torque tube and prop shaft, improved exhaust system mounts, stiffer clutch springs, and a new six-spline transmission mainshaft (versus 18 splines) ground to center the second- and third-gear synchros more accurately. Chevrolet would stay with vacuum gearshift through 1948, and torque-tube drive through 1954.

The rear spring rates were reduced so they almost matched the fronts, providing a flatter and smoother ride. Springs were relocated further outboard for greater stability, and in 1940 the shackles had been angled so the spring rates increased as load went up. These were Chevy's so-called "tension shackles," an idea adopted by Ford in 1949.

Special De Luxe Five-Passenger Coupe
IN TWO-TONE COLOR COMBINATION

1941 Special DeLuxe five-passenger coupe (with optional two-tone paint)

Most Chevrolet accessories for 1941 were dealer-installed. Salesmen sold them from an attractive two-color folder that suggested owners opt for additional items from season to season. The passage of some 40 inflationary years makes these accessories seem like bargains today. Here are a few examples. Directional signals cost $7.90; a vacuum-powered windshield washer was available for $2.95. A front-bumper grille guard cost $6.25; rear bumper "wing tip" guards were $2.50 the set; a trunk guard "sufficiently strong to permit the car to be pushed" could be ordered for $3.50. Unusual accessories included a "No-Rol" device, similar to Studebaker's "Hill Holder," that prevented the car from rolling backward when declutched on a hill. No-Rol cost the buyer $8.75. Finally, for those who had to have everything, 85 cents would add an emergency brake release signal that emitted "a pleasing sound".

Chevrolet's accessory "washboard" front fender trim ($4) had an interesting origin. According to Ned Nickles, "The chrome on the fenders was part of Harley Earl's theory on brightness—and it served a useful function, too. The panels helped conceal wavy fenders after accident repairs. But Earl had another reason for this accessory. When a Chevy went on the used-car market, the trim panels kept it from looking dull. There was still some brightness, some life to it."

The 1941 Chevy lineup was as follows:

Body style	Price	Production
Master DeLuxe		
business coupe	$712	48,763
coupe	743	79,124
Town Sedan, 2d	754	219,438
Sport Sedan, 4d	795	59,538
Special DeLuxe		
business coupe	$769	17,602

Body style	Price	Production
coupe	800	155,889
cabriolet (conv)	949	15,296
Town Sedan, 2d	810	228,458
Sport Sedan, 4d	851	148,661
station wagon	995	2,045
Fleetline sedan	877	34,162

Surprising to many modern students of the marque, Chevy two-doors outsold four-doors in these years. The rarest model was, not unexpectedly, the lovely woody wagon. The Fleetline sedan, a fastback introduced midway through the model year, sold quite well in the few months before the '42s appeared. An unusual midyear offering was the choice of special green or blue interiors at slight extra cost. Introduced in April, Chevys so equipped were known as "Easter cars." The trim was available on the Special Deluxe Town Sedan, Sport Sedan, and five-passenger coupe. In addition, customers automatically received woodgrain dash and garnish moldings, a feature originally introduced on the Fleetline fastback. There are only a few "Easter cars" still around, and they are highly prized today.

Speaking only of perfectly restored or prime original specimens, the 1941 Chevrolet (and its rarer 1942 cousin) are the most sought-after versions of the 1940–48 generation. A mint-condition convertible can cost as much as $9000. Woody wagons, despite their rarity, run about $2000 less, while other Special DeLuxe models can fetch up to $4000. Masters are somewhat less expensive. It is interesting to note that despite the scarcity of the 1942s, prices for '41s on today's collector market are equal or higher. If nothing else, it goes to prove that today as yesterday, the '41 Chevy has just what a lot of America wants.

One of the rare '42s—the Special DeLuxe business coupe

1949: Last of the Woodies—First of a New Breed of Chevys

By the end of the 1940s, the American automobile industry was changing its ideas about the station wagon. Up through World War II, "suburbans," as they were first called, were heavy, ungainly vehicles designed principally as cargo haulers. Their wooden bodies were most often manufactured by special builders like Hercules and Cantrell, and mounted on bare chassis and cowl assemblies supplied by the car companies. But despite their clumsiness, these wagons displayed workmanship that was beyond reproach: corners beautifully curved, mahogany panels perfectly inset between strips of ash or northern birch, structural members exquisitely mitred together. Such craftsmanship makes the traditional "woody" an *object d'art* among collectors today.

These enthusiasts might think woodies less desirable had they lived with the cars when new. In their day, the woody suburbans suffered several nagging problems. For instance, the bodies required a lot of periodic maintenance. Regular revarnishing and careful attention to joints and seams was a must—especially if the car had to spend any time outdoors. Their canvas-over-wood tops shrank, cracked, and fractured easily. Because of the expensive semi-hand construction involved, wagons were the highest-priced models in the line. They were also the heaviest, which meant poorer fuel economy than their linemates. They rattled and leaked, and felt awkward on the move. The rearmost seat was usually bolted to the floor, and had to be manhandled out of the car when extra cargo room was required. Inevitably, all these impractical features forced automakers to develop more practical station wagon designs.

The first significant improvement came with Chrysler's relatively streamlined Town & Country of 1941–42. With its smoothly curved roof and side-hinged "clamshell" rear doors, the Town & Country was better-looking than any other suburban on the market, and more practical to enter from the rear. Its rear-door arrangement forecast the two-way tailgates of the 1960s.

After the war, Willys-Overland committed itself to Jeep-like vehicles and won considerable success with its all-steel station wagons. Though more of a truck than a car, the appealing Jeep Suburban and Station Sedan proved that steel construction was lighter, cheaper, and easier to maintain than a wood body.

Other manufacturers took note of Willys, and began conjuring their own replacements for the traditional woody. Starting with Packard's Station Sedan of 1948, the use of wood as a structural material became less and less common. On the Packard, wood appeared as trim on the doors, but was structural only around the tailgate.

In 1949, two interesting alternatives to the station wagon appeared: DeSoto bowed with the Carry-All, and Kaiser debuted its Traveler and Vagabond. All three looked like (and were based on) conventional sedans, but had rear seats that could be folded down to create huge, flat beds. The Traveler and Vagabond featured a double rear hatch (separate liftgate and tailgate) for rear access and an extended cargo floor. The DeSoto had a conventional decklid, but there

1948 Fleetmaster wood-bodied station wagon

22

1949 Styleline DeLuxe
wood-bodied station wagon

was no fixed bulkhead between its trunk compartment and the interior. Ultimately, buyers found squareback wagons more useful than either of these halfway measures. Yet, DeSoto and Kaiser pioneered folding rear seats for other U.S. automakers, which adopted the idea widely in the '60s, along with the hatchback.

A more fundamental change in wagon design also occurred in 1949: Chevrolet, Plymouth, Oldsmobile, and Pontiac each introduced station wagons with all-steel construction midway through the model year. Though the 1949 Plymouth Suburban is usually cited as the first wagon based on a conventional passenger car bodyshell, the GM versions appeared at the

same time and were similarly conceived. All four were first shown in the spring of 1949. In Plymouth's case, the Suburban was part of a complete restyling effort; in the case of the GM cars, the steel wagons replaced the woodies introduced the previous autumn.

Plymouth made no pretenses about the Suburban's contruction: there wasn't anything on it that even suggested wood. The all-steel Chevrolet, Pontiac, and Oldsmobile wagons, however, looked much like their woody predecessors. In place of wooden

Kaiser's 1949 Vagabond

Plymouth's all-steel 1949 Suburban

1949 Styleline DeLuxe wood-bodied station wagon

trim and structural members was metal painted to look like wood. Up close, the difference was more obvious: the light-colored simulated woodwork curved around windows and tailgate while the northern birch of the true wood-bodied cars was square-cut.

Oldsmobile offered two wagons, a six-cylinder Series 76 and a V-8 Series 88, priced at $2895 and $3295, respectively. Pontiac had four woodies: Streamliner and Streamliner Deluxe versions available with either six-cylinder or straight-eight engines. The most expensive of the quartet sold for $2690. When steel-bodied look-alikes replaced the woodies, Olds and Pontiac stayed with these relatively high prices, though it certainly cost much less to build the all-steel cars. In 1950, however, both divisions dropped wagon prices by about $300 across the board.

Chevrolet followed the pricing policy of its sister divisions, but had only one wagon in its line, part of the DeLuxe Styleline series. The price of $2267 applied to both the original woody and its steel-bodied replacement. Like Olds and Pontiac, Chevy reduced this rather high figure after the 1950 models appeared.

At $1855, the Suburban had a strong price advantage over the GM wagons, and Plymouth sold over 19,000 in 1949. Pontiac and Oldsmobile wagon production was miniscule by comparison, not more than 3000 each. Chevrolet built 3342 woody wagons for the model year, followed by 6006 of their all-steel replacements. So the '49 woody wagon is one of the rarest postwar Chevys. There are probably fewer than a dozen still in existence.

Chevrolet's last woody was certainly its best. The year 1949 marked the first all-new styling at GM since the war, and Harley Earl's sleek new shape resulted in one of the most attractive Chevy lineups in years. The separate fender concept wasn't totally abandoned for the new models—rear fenders still bolted on the time-honored manner. But the trend toward the full-envelope body was obvious. Low front fenders swept back smoothly to a clean, rounded deck. The grille was a modest affair, composed of horizontal and vertical bars. For sedan buyers, both notchbacks and fastbacks were offered. The Fleetline two-door fastback was the most dramatic-looking product among the "low-priced three" that year, and was not unlike the great Bentley Continentals of the mid- and late '50s in appearance.

Interiors were also changed for 1949. Chevrolet abandoned its traditional symmetrical dashboard and now clustered instruments in a circular pod ahead of the steering wheel. A central radio grille was flanked at the right by a clock and a flush-fitting glovebox lid. DeLuxe models came with dual sunvisors, clock, and cigarette lighter as standard equipment.

Although the 1949 Chevrolet's 115-inch wheelbase was actually an inch shorter than that of its predecessor, its low, svelte styling made it look much longer. The new two-piece windshield was curved, and was 2.5 inches lower than on the 1948 car. Advantages of the 1949 restyle are especially evident when comparing station wagons. The 1948 and earlier Chevy woodies were typical of the old breed—high, boxy, heavy-looking, and dumpy. The 1949 woody was entirely different.

In construction, Chevrolet, like Packard, made minimal use of wood as a structural material, so its wagons featured a steel roof panel and steel sides. The woodwork, furnished by the Ionia Company, started around the door windows, and flared out and back along the rear fenderline. The tailgate and lift-up rear window frame were made of wood, but the only structural wooden elements were the vertical supports at the rear corners of the body. These were joined to the steel roof pillars at the beltline. The liftgate's hinges were exposed, while those on the drop-down tailgate were hidden to give a smooth appearance. There was only one taillamp, which also served to illuminate the license plate. The assembly was designed to swing down so the taillight and plate would be visible with the tailgate lowered.

On the inside, Chevrolet's woody parted company with previous wagons with appointments very much like those of the '49 sedans. Instead of the usual wooden door panels and slatted canvas-over-wood headliner, there were upholstered door trims and a conventional headliner. Because it was more likely to see heavy-duty use than a sedan, the wagon had standard vinyl upholstery instead of cloth.

In accessibility, the Chevy wagon was clearly superior to the Plymouth. For one thing, it had four doors, making rear seat entry and exit easier than in the two-door Suburban. Engineers provided more cargo area room by moving the spare to a compartment under the floor. Like most wagons of the day, the Chevy's tailgate, when lowered, could be used to extend the length of the cargo floor for carrying extra-long loads.

Out on the road, the 1949 woody was much better than its predecessor. Suspension revisions and a lower center of gravity had made the '49 one of the best-handling Chevrolets ever—and better than its Plymouth and Ford rivals. All the new models were beautifully put together. The precise fit of body panels, the car's tight feeling over rough surfaces, the way the shift lever snicked cleanly through the gears, and the positive response to controls all reflected the extremes taken by engineers to make the design "right."

Despite their revolutionary new body and chassis design, Chevrolet left the engine department basically unaltered for its '49 models. The tried-and-true 216.5 cubic-inch overhead-valve six (bore and stroke 3.25 × 3.75) was carried over from 1948, still producing 90 brake horsepower at 3300 rpm. Overdrive was available as a dealer-installed option, but two-speed Powerglide automatic was still a year away. Model year production was 1,037,600, consisting of 769,893 DeLuxe models and 267,707 Specials. Calendar year production, at 1,109,958 units, was the second highest in Chevrolet history—not close to 1927's banner 1.75 million, but encouraging nonetheless. In the production race, Chevy once again overwhelmed Ford (840,000 units) and produced nearly twice as many cars as Plymouth (575,000).

Management changes at Chevrolet had been

1949 DeLuxe Styleline Sport Sedan

occurring rapidly since 1946. In June of that year, M. E. Coyle was replaced as division general manager by Nicholas Dreystadt, previously general manager of Cadillac. Dreystadt immediately embarked on a production "push" that sent Chevy from about 400,000 units in calendar 1946 to the million-plus of 1949. Unfortunately, Dreystadt wasn't around to see the final results: he succumbed to cancer in 1948. His replacement, W. W. Armstrong, also became ill, and was succeeded by Thomas H. Keating in 1949. After that, the division went from strength to strength. Under Keating, Chevrolet engineering was headed by Edward H. Kelley, who was relieved in 1952 by the redoubtable Edward N. Cole, father of the 1955 V-8.

The 1949 model may thus be considered a watershed for Chevrolet. It symbolized the swift design and engineering advances being made throughout the industry after the war, and also marked the arrival of the new Keating administration with its optimism about Chevy's future as America's number-one seller. Ahead lay several years of careful consolidation; rising production, pushing the 1.5 million mark in many years; more emphasis on engineering; and additional body styles. One of these was destined to reshape America's attitude about convertibles as much as the all-steel wagon had changed buyer thinking about woodies. This was the 1950 Bel Air—first of the Chevy hardtops.

1949 DeLuxe Styleline wood-bodied station wagon

25

Bel Air: Chevrolet's First Hardtop

By 1949, the auto industry had been wrestling with "Jekyll-and-Hyde" open body styles for two generations. Convertibles were great—about 10 percent of the time. But in less-than-perfect weather they were leaky, drafty, often downright chilly—especially in the days before modern car heaters. In the Teens, many wealthy car owners maintained a chassis and *two* bodies—an open model for the summer months, a sedan for the winter. Bodies would be laboriously switched every spring and fall. This tiresome business gave rise to the "California" or "all-season" top. This was a bolt-on affair upholstered in fabric or leather, which could be fitted to an open touring body—much like today's steel and fiberglass accessory tops designed to substitute for the folding roof on small sports cars.

As the automobile became more complex and expensive, such solutions to civilizing the open car became less desirable. After World War II, the advent of better roads and higher speeds made open-air driving even less practical than before. Yet almost everyone agreed that the open body style was the most stylish and entertaining way to go motoring. How then to achieve both sportiness and comfort in one car? Enter the "hardtop-convertible."

Chrysler holds title to the first "production" hard-top. In 1946, designers took the steel roof from a club coupe and wedded it to the Town & Country convertible, retaining the ragtop's pillarless side window construction. This provided much of the open-air feel of a true convertible, while allowing the car to be buttoned up securely in foul weather. But the Town & Country hardtops were little more than experiments: only seven were built, all in 1946.

Kaiser-Frazer hatched another of its unusual ideas with the 1949 Kaiser Virginian, a "Hard Top" introduced in late 1948. Like the Town & Country, the Virginian was basically a convertible with a steel top grafted on. It was unique for its day in having four doors—but at close to $3000, it hardly sold well. K-F built about 1000 for 1949–50, along with 152 Frazer Manhattans built from leftover Virginians for the 1951 model year.

The company that really put the hardtop-convertible on the automotive map was none other than General Motors. GM was the styling leader in the early postwar days (as it is now), and Harley Earl's staff at the Art & Colour Studio was thinking about hardtops even before the war ended. After V-J day, GM's prewar models were freshened up slightly and returned to fill in while the company readied its corporate-wide redesign for 1949. Among these first all-

Kaiser's 1949 Virginian (originally "Hard Top")

1949 Cadillac Coupe deVille

Interior of the 1950 Bel Air

new postwar cars were three hardtops: the Cadillac 62 Coupe deVille, the Oldsmobile 98 Holiday, and the Buick Roadmaster Riviera.

All three were trimmed as luxuriously as their convertible counterparts. This included the highest-quality upholstery, often leather; headliners trimmed with bright metal ribs to simulate the look of a raised convertible top; and rear windows wrapped smartly around at the sides. Introduced late in the model year, these first hardtops sold modestly: 4343 Riv-

1949 Buick Roadmaster Riviera

ieras, 2150 Coupes deVille, and 3006 Holidays. But they started a trend. In the early '50s, the hardtop proliferated throughout the industry. By the end of that decade, it had almost displaced the two-door sedan as America's favorite body type, and had put a severe dent in convertible sales. In 1955, the idea spread to four-door models, and there were even hardtop station wagons by 1957.

With the lower volume and break-even point at Buick, Olds, and Cadillac, it was logical these divisions be the first to offer hardtops as a way to "test the waters." Once GM's product planners were satisfied that public reception was favorable, they called for Chevrolet and Pontiac hardtops in 1950. As with its all-steel wagons, Pontiac initially offered no less than four hardtops, all called Catalina: Chieftain DeLuxe and Super Deluxe, each available with a choice of six or eight cylinders. Chevrolet, on the other hand, offered only one—in the DeLuxe Styleline series—called Bel Air. But with 74,634 sales, it outsold all the Catalinas put together.

The 1950 Chevrolet line was the second year for the then-current styling cycle, and accordingly was changed only mildly from 1949. Appearance alterations included two heavy, vertical chevron-design grille bars directly below the parking lights and a crescent-shaped "wing" attached to the hood em-

1950 DeLuxe Bel Air hardtop coupe

blem. Fastbacks were continued under the Fleetline label in both Special and DeLuxe trim. Notchback sedans and coupes, plus a wagon, convertible, and the Bel Air hardtop made up the Styleline series. The Bel Air sold for $1741, about $100 less than the Chevy convertible and some $250 more than the sport coupe.

In construction, the Bel Air hardtop looked exactly like other Styleline models from the beltline down. Convertible-type frame reinforcements were used to make up for the loss of structural rigidity due to lack of a conventional B-pillar. A small amount of flex in the doorpost area was typical of early hardtops. Indeed, *Motor Trend,* in its 19th issue, suggested that the Bel Air "sacrifices practicality merely to achieve the esthetic styling of a convertible. If the metal top on the Bel Air were made removable (held on by a number of clamps at convenient locations), this body design would then be both esthetic *and* practical." One wonders if *Motor Trend* was really serious. In any event, nobody in the industry ever considered making the huge steel roofs of full-size hardtops removable.

Chevrolet interiors were never very elaborate in those days, but the Bel Air's was plusher than most. Instead of broadcloth, the new hardtop was upholstered in a combination of genuine leather and pile-cord fabric. Like the Riviera, Catalina, Coupe deVille, and Holiday, it featured bright metal roof bows in the headliner to provide the feel of a true convertible. With its windows rolled down, the Bel Air was completely pillarless, though engineers found it necessary for weather protection to install little hinged metal flaps where the side windows met the roof.

Sharing the spotlight with the Bel Air hardtop for 1950 was another important innovation for Chevrolet, two-speed Powerglide automatic transmission. This consisted of a five-element torque converter, with maximum torque multiplication of 2.2:1, combined with a planetary gearset for reverse and emergency low. The five torque-multiplying elements worked in tandem, providing variable ratios to suit all driving conditions without the need to change gears. Indeed, the transmission didn't shift unless the driver selected the "Low" range manually. Car magazine road testers complained about this, and suggested that a kickdown detent be installed, something that was done in later years. *Motor Trend* definitely preferred the standard-shift Chevy: "For the person who doesn't mind shifting, the standard transmission is better; for the one who likes to do no more driving than just step on the throttle and brake, the Powerglide enjoys the advantage."

A prominent *dis*advantage of Powerglide was that it soaked up a certain amount of engine power. To compensate, Chevrolet developed a 105-bhp version of its sturdy six. Manual cars were equipped with the old 216.5-cid unit, yielding 92 brake horsepower at 3400 rpm. Powerglide models got a bored and

1950 Styleline DeLuxe four-door sedan

stroked 325.5-cid engine (3.56×3.93) with hydraulic valve lifters and a higher-lift cam. Other features of the 105-bhp six were its better breathing via larger intake valves, ports, and manifold passages; a larger cylinder head, with provision for still higher compression than 1950's 6.7:1; a stronger block, with thicker cylinder walls and an additional rib compared to the smaller six; and oil grooves in the side of piston bushings that distributed oil in low pressure areas.

Chevrolet was no performance car in 1950, and wouldn't be for another five years. Against a 0-60 mph acceleration time of 19.8 seconds with manual transmission, *Motor Trend* recorded 27.5 seconds with Powerglide, using Drive range only. This was reduced to 21.8 seconds by starting in Low and shifting manually to Drive. In the standing-start quarter-mile, the manual and Powerglide cars were only about 1.5 seconds apart, suggesting that "the pick-up of the Powerglide at medium speed ranges is somewhat better than the conventional-transmission car." Despite its sleek looks, the Bel Air was less slippery than other Chevys due to its relatively high roofline. Its top speed of 89 mph could probably have been bettered by a Fleetline fastback. Top speed of equivalent body styles with Powerglide, however, was slightly higher than with the manual gearbox, which pulled a 4.11 rear axle ratio, against Powerglide's 3.55:1. There were no optional ratios, though overdrive was still offered as a dealer-installed item.

If 1949 had been a good year for Chevy, 1950 was even better. Calendar year production hit 1.5 million, about 330,000 units more than Ford and nearly a million more than Plymouth. Neither of Chevy's two main competitors had a hardtop yet, though both would add one the following season—Ford the Victoria and Plymouth the Belvedere. It is logical to assume that the Bel Air's 74,000 sales in 1950 represented the total low-priced hardtop market that year. How different from ten years later, when hardtops would take over 35 percent of new-car sales.

The 1950 Bel Air was certainly a car of compromises. It had to be because it was built to a price,

perhaps more so than GM's other hardtops. This implied certain shortcomings that would have been eliminated for a car priced at $2200, like the Pontiac Catalina. Although $1741 sounds ridiculously cheap by today's inflated standards, it was far more than anyone expected to pay for a Chevy 30 years ago. The cheapest model in the 1950 line, the Special Styleline business coupe, cost only $1329; the four-door sedan was tagged at a mere $1450. And the dollar was worth maybe four times what it's worth today.

The verdict returned on the 1950 Bel Air by contemporary road testers was virtually unanimous. Its best features were the smooth styling, extremely tight body, low upkeep costs, ease of resale, and good handling. Chevys had been very roadable cars beginning with the all-new 1949 models, and offered nimble handling aided by quick, positive steering. (The 1950 model had a steering ratio of only 17.4:1.) The hardtop's advantages, aside from the open-air feel it imparted, were slightly more luxury and extremely good visibility. It had more glass area than any other Chevy body type, and was quite "glassy" for the day. Design drawbacks included marginal brakes (self-aligning 11-inch hydraulic drums) and a harder ride than either Ford or Plymouth. The Bel Air may have been pricey for a Chevrolet, but there wasn't another car in the lineup quite like it—let alone in those of its two chief rivals.

It all added up to an attractive, salable package, and Bel Airs continued to move well for the next several years. Chevrolet churned out over 100,000 of the 1951 and 1953 versions. The 1952s would have been as plentiful were it not for production restrictions caused by the Korean war (output that year was about 75,000).

Perhaps the most significant thing about the Bel Air was its sportiness. Chevys had never been really interesting cars before (except perhaps for convertibles), and inevitably had spewed forth from the production line in a profusion of mundane body styles.

All Chevrolet really needed now was performance to match its cars' new-found good looks. Ed Cole would take care of that in 1955.

1950 DeLuxe Bel Air hardtop coupe

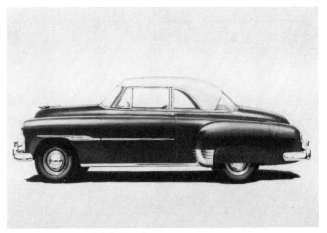

1951 DeLuxe Bel Air hardtop coupe

Nomad: A Revolution and a Landmark Year

It will always be remembered as a blue-ribbon year. The combination of Ed Cole's powerful small-block 265 V-8, sensational new styling, and the highest sales in the history of the industry to that time made 1955 a landmark for Chevrolet. So were its cars. Its first V-8 in 35 years was a bold and successful answer to Ford in the performance sweepstakes. A Ferrari-inspired grille and rakish two-toning highlighted the new sheetmetal, singular and unmistakable, wrapped around that engine. Production of over 1.7 million vehicles for the model year insured that the '55s would still be around 25 years later to be remembered by a new generation of enthusiasts. In fact, Chevrolet's smashing output of over six million 1955–57 models means that enough survive today for 15,000 collectors to enjoy what has come to be known as the "classic Chevy."

It is perhaps misleading to single out one particular model in the 1955 line for special treatment. All three series, the Bel Air in particular, deserve strong acclaim. But if any one model symbolizes Chevy's design and engineering innovations for '55, it would have to be the Bel Air Nomad station wagon.

Though Chevrolet shared the spotlight in the development of all-steel wagons in 1949, it stood alone with the Nomad. Here, for the first time, was a car that combined the luxury and airiness of a hardtop with the practicality of a station wagon. True, Pontiac fielded its similar Safari that same year, but it was derived from Chevrolet's idea and lacked the Nomad's impact.

Although the station wagon and the hardtop evolved separately after the war, it was left to Chevrolet with its vast resources to combine these two

The first Bel Air Nomad—a stand-out in Chevy's landmark 1955 line

1954 Corvette Nomad show car

concepts in one car. On the face of it, the idea made sense. From a few thousand in 1949, the hardtop body style had become so popular that, by 1955, it accounted for nearly a fifth of the market. Station wagons, which represented 2.8 percent of production in 1948, had risen to nearly 15 percent by the mid-'50s. Considering these numbers, it's easy to understand how Chevrolet management would conclude that a wagon with hardtop styling couldn't miss. The result was perhaps the prettiest station wagon ever to roll off an assembly line.

Chevrolet wasn't the only one toying with the idea.

Willys had planned a pretty two-door hardtop wagon for its 1955 Aero line, but ended passenger-car production before the car could be realized. Chrysler displayed two novel hardtop-wagon show cars—the two-door Plainsman in 1956 and the four-door Plymouth Cabana in 1958. Even Rambler offered a four-door hardtop-wagon, the Cross Country of 1956, copping a "first" that is all but forgotten today. But the Nomad is far better remembered than any of these.

Like many great Chevys, this one started as a dream car for one of General Motors' popular Moto-

Timeless styling and the most imaginative wagon ever—the 1955 Bel Air Nomad

The dream car that reached production poses for a typical mid-'50s publicity photo.

ramas. As Chevy designer Clare MacKichan remembers, it was based on none other than the Corvette: "As far as I can recall, Mr. Earl should get the credit for suggesting it . . . A young man named Carl Renner, who was working in a special studio, had come up with a sketch for a station wagon roof that caught Earl's eye." The result was a Corvette front end grafted onto a fiberglass two-door wagon body, mounted on a 1953 Chevrolet station wagon chassis. Renner's unique embellishments for the "Corvette Nomad" were its sporty roofline with wrapped side windows, and a distinctive, wide, slanted B-pillar. The show car's rear window disappeared completely into the tailgate, a feature that did not appear in regular production until 1959.

Originally, the car was finished in white fiberglass, but for the 1954 Motorama the lower body was painted blue (Harley Earl's favorite color) to contrast with the white roof. Only one Corvette Nomad was built, a non-running display piece. According to MacKichan, it "was scrapped sometime in the 1960s and no longer exists. Persistent stories crop up from time to time that we have it squirreled away in a warehouse somewhere in Detroit, but unfortunately this seems to be a myth."

When the car was shown, crowds raved about its styling, and Harley Earl's friends told him what a brilliant idea it was. Earl's manager, Howard O'Leary, called MacKichan from the Motorama. "When I get back in two days I want to see that whole car, and how you would do it on a '55 Chevrolet," O'Leary reportedly said.

Excitement swept the Chevrolet studio at the prospect of turning an experimental "dream car" design into production reality. Renner set to work. Said MacKichan: "The Nomad roof was taken from a full-size drawing, cut apart, stretched out and mated to the basic design of the 1955 Chevrolet lower body,

windshield, etc.; which was done in the body design studio. The innovations of the Corvette Nomad were carried into the production car, introduced in February 1955. The hardtop front door glass framing, the forward-sloping rear quarters, the wide B-pillar, the fluted roof, the wraparound rear side glass, the rear wheel cutout, and the seven vertical accent strips on the tailgate were all retained in a remarkably good translation from the dream car." (The vertical tailgate strips, nicknamed "bananas" by Nomad lovers, formed a sort of nerf-type bumper on the original show car.)

There's an interesting story concerning the fluted roof. Originally, Earl fancied a stainless-steel telescoping roof section, which could be retracted for partial open-air motoring at the touch of a button or the turn of a crank. Had this made production, the Nomad would have been a three-way combination: hardtop, wagon, and "convertible." But production costs and worries about leaks precluded it, though the fluting was retained as a visual suggestion of the intended design. Eight year later, thanks to the work of Brooks Stevens, Studebaker would produce a wagon with a sliding rear roof section that worked like a steel sunroof rather than a telescope.

Renner recounts the process of mating the show car styling with the production body: "It went quite fast, taking that roof and adapting it, jockeying around to match the production version, step by step. But there again [we had] good leadership and good decisions. We went ahead." Since work didn't begin until January 1954—long after the '55 styling had been locked up—the Nomad did not appear with the rest of the line in October. The production version was first shown, alongside Pontiac's Safari, at the 1955 Motorama in New York City. (Pontiac insisted

continued on page 41

Great Cars From
Chevrolet
COLOR SHOWCASE I

1914 Series H Royal Mail roadster

1932 Confederate Series BA DeLuxe five-window, four-passenger Sport Coupe

1941 Special DeLuxe cabriolet (convertible)

Above: 1948 Fleetline Aerosedan

Below: 1949 Styleline DeLuxe wood-body station wagon

Above: 1949 Styleline DeLuxe wood-body station wagon

Below: 1955 Bel Air hardtop coupe

1955 Bel Air convertible

1955 Bel Air Nomad hardtop wagon

39

Above: 1956 Bel Air convertible

Below: 1956 Bel Air hardtop coupe

Except for front end, Nomad shared little exterior sheetmetal with other '55 Chevys like this Two-Ten hardtop coupe.

continued from page 32

on having its own version of the Nomad after its managers saw it, much to the chagrin of Chevrolet Division.)

Approximately 300 Nomads were built, partially by hand, for display at dealerships and shows in early 1955. Though no one knows for sure, many researchers believe these pilot cars differed from later, true production models in two details: a handle on the center tailgate strip and an outside reveal molding around the rear quarter windows.

While the Nomad was visually related to other '55 Chevys, it shared little sheetmetal with them from the cowl back. Doors were hardtop-styled, but differed slightly from the standard configuration since the Nomad had no beltline dip. Quarter panels were unique because of the Nomad's higher rear wheel cutouts as well as its straight beltline. The floor was shared with the standard two-door station wagon. Tail- and liftgates also differed from those of the regular wagons. The Nomad liftgate had a heavy, chrome-plated, die-cast metal frame. The tailgate, with its chrome "bananas," carried the Nomad name in script near its upper edge just below the liftgate. In profile, the Nomad's rear end was more raked than that of the regular wagons. Its roofline, B- and C-pillars were, of course, exclusive to it.

The Nomad wore no rear quarter panel trim as on the rest of the Bel Air series; its Chevrolet emblem

Pontiac got its own version of the Nomad over Chevrolet's objections. Here's the '56 edition of the Safari.

1956 Rambler Cross Country four-door hardtop-wagon

1955 Bel Air Nomad

and Bel Air script were positioned on the rear fenders, just aft of the fuel filler flap. Taillamps were stock 1955 units and the rear bumper was shared with other '55 wagons. Inside, linoleum covered the rear deck area, also as in the standard wagons. The headliner was vinyl, decorated with chrome bows.

The '55 model also had four touches not found on its 1956 and '57 successors: chrome headlamp trim, front fender and door moldings, a special interior, and an individual rear wheel cutout design. The trim pieces, created by Chevy's Bob Veryzer, set the Nomad apart from the rest of the '55 line. The insert formed by the side molding was painted white just like the rear fender trim on other Bel Air models.

A waffle-rib vinyl was used on the Nomad's seats. Door and side panels were covered in an attractive combination of plain and waffle-pattern vinyl. Interestingly, the 1956–57 Corvette was upholstered with a similar waffle-design material.

After 1955, Nomads shared the standard Bel Air in-

terior and had no unique exterior trim. This parts standardization was an attempt to reduce the car's high production costs, which perhaps explained its low sales. By the time Chevy began tooling up for 1956, the future of the distinctive Nomad was in some doubt, mainly because only 8530 copies of the '55 had been sold. Chevrolet gambled and continued the Nomad for 1956 and '57 when just 8103 and 6534, respectively, were sold—ridiculously low volume by Chevy standards.

The primary problem was the assumption that just because hardtops and station wagons were popular, a hardtop-wagon would be, too. And in some ways, the Nomad was easy to resist. First, it carried the highest price in the Chevy line, $2571 with V-8 engine. That was $200 more than the Bel Air four-door wagon, and $265 more than the convertible. For that money, the buyer got only two doors, which never appealed as much to utility-minded wagon buyers as four-door models. Second, there were several detail

Nomad was continued for '56 but was now identical with the rest of the line except for its roof.

problems with the design. Though the Nomad's glassy greenhouse provided exceptional visibility, it made the car pretty hot on sunny days. Air circulation through the sliding rear windows wasn't the best either. Factory air conditioning cost $565, an almost prohibitive sum for 1955. The liftgate was designed so that, when open, exhaust fumes were sucked back inside. Even with the rear gates closed, rain leaks were common.

Thus, the Nomad passed into history, a rather noble oddity. But the hardtop-wagon idea, which it so brilliantly expressed, didn't die. In 1957 came the Buick Caballero and Oldsmobile Fiesta—both pillarless hardtop-wagons with *four* doors. These sold well. That same year, a two-door hardtop-wagon was added to the Mercury line. In 1960, after the GM and Ford versions were dropped, Chrysler took up the slack with its Town & Country four-doors in both the Windsor and New Yorker series. Along with their Dodge counterparts, these were sold through 1964.

In summary, the hardtop-wagon should be considered as a necessary step in automotive design evolution. The station wagon no longer commands as much of the market as it did in the '50s, but it is still quite popular. The Nomad was almost certainly the most imaginative and stylish example of what had been a boring body style. It proved even practical cars could be exciting.

No story about any '55 Chevy would be complete without comment on Ed Cole's 265 cubic-inch V-8. It set the pattern for Chevy's future performance engines, and is respected today as one of the best powerplants ever. Cole had decided to go ahead with this engine as soon as he arrived to head Chevrolet Engineering in 1952. His predecessor, E. H. Kelley, had considered a 231 cubic-inch V-8 and even a V-6; both were shelved. "We knew that a certain bore/stroke relationship was the most compact," Cole said. "We knew we'd like a displacement of 265 cubic inches, and that automatically established the bore and stroke [3.75 × 3.00 inches]. And we never changed any of this."

Though this 162- to 180-bhp V-8 was a brand-new design, it adhered to certain fundamentals. Since it would be a Chevrolet unit, it had to be simple in construction, economical to build, and efficient to run. One feature that points up how well the engineers met these goals was its lack of a common rocker arm shaft. Each rocker arm was independent of the others, so that deflection of one had no effect on any other. Each was assembled over a valve stem and pushrod, retained by a fulcrum ball and lock nut. Regardless of whether mechanical or hydraulic valve lifters were used, the valves were lashed by turning the lock nut. This reduced reciprocating weight, which in turn allowed higher rpm.

The intake manifold provided a common water outlet to both heads, which were die-cast with integral valve guides and completely interchangeable. This valve train arrangement was shared with Pontiac, which designed a slightly larger V-8 along similar principles. A short-stroke engine meant short connecting rods. Pressed-in piston pins eliminated the need to slit the rod and the need for a locking bolt. Five main bearings carried the maximum loads in their lower halves.

Further weight saving was accomplished by circulating the oil through hollow pushrods. This provided splash-lube to the rockers and valve stems without separate and costly oil lines. Details included an "autothermic" slipper-type aluminum piston with three rings and a circumferential expander for its single oil ring. Instead of alloy iron, the crankshaft was made of forged steel for its higher specific gravity and modulus of elasticity. A new forging process allowed Chevrolet to reduce overall crankshaft length. A chart of the engine's torsional vibration periods showed very low peaks and few sharp points throughout most of the rev range. Adding a harmonic balancer eliminated most of the remaining torsional vibration.

The exhaust manifolds were routed near the top of the cylinder heads, with exhaust passages pointing upward and out. The entire length of the ports was water-jacketed. Chevrolet switched to a 12-volt electrical system for this engine, as six-volt systems didn't prove to have the voltage needed for a high-compression powerplant. The 12-volt system also provided more efficient generator output, better steering operation, and allowed the use of smaller-gauge wires and cables. Overall, the 265 was a very light engine—it weighed 40 pounds less than the Chevy six, and was much lighter than Studebaker's comparable 259.

Of course the whole concept of the '55 Chevy revolved around lightness. Said Ed Cole: "We got away from the heavy torque-tube drive and went to Hotchkiss drive. We went to a Salisbury-type axle instead of the banjo-type. Then we went to ball-joint front suspension for weight saving. And we went to a tubular frame. It was a brand-new engine and a brand-new body, too. Today, if you wanted to take the same sort of risk at Chevrolet, you'd promptly be fired."

This milestone engine design was certainly one of the most important of all time. Yet, it was only one component in a thoroughly impressive overall package. The 1955 Chevrolet, deftly designed by people like Clare MacKichan, Carl Renner, and Bob Veryzer, was a fine-looking automobile. Its eggcrate grille, lithe lines, and colorful interior made the car almost irresistible. And it was introduced with an almost uncanny sense of timing—1955 was, after all, a great year for selling cars. Everybody did well. Ford ran a close race, but in the end, Chevy triumphed with 1,830,029 cars against Ford's 1,764,524. In model year production, Chevrolet looked even better with 1,704,667 units against Ford's 1,451,157. So 1955 belonged to Chevy—and for all the right reasons.

Corvette: The Coming of Age, 1956-57

The Corvette came very close to extinction in 1955, when only 700 were produced. The "first-generation" 1953–55 car had been criticized by the purists for its overdone styling. In particular, barbs were aimed at the taillights that sprouted rocket-like from the rear fenders, and the bulbous shape—not to mention the anemic six-cylinder engine and two-speed automatic transmission. For a time, General

1955 Corvette

LaSalle II hardtop show car at '55 Motorama

Motors had reservations about continuing the Corvette. After all, it had made the attempt at an American sports car, and a lot of company insiders expressed willingness to let it fade into history. What happened to change their minds can be summed up in one word—Thunderbird.

Ford's two-seat "boulevard sports car" arrived at the height of the perennial sales war between the two industry giants. For 18 months beginning in mid-1953, Ford and Chevy slugged it out, swamping their dealers with unordered cars. The dealers were forced to sell them at almost any price or be financially buried by the avalanche. Henry Ford II was determined, he said, to become number-one in the industry, even if he had to *give* his cars away. GM naturally responded, and the battle was on. Both companies took to the media to claim victory, then made counterclaims and accused each other of fudging statistics. The final figures said Chevy was the winner in 1955 production—by a hair. But the finish was close enough to change GM's attitude about the Corvette, and the decision was made to keep it in production. Basically, it was a matter of pride: GM was not about to leave the two-seater field because of the T-Bird. As a result, ads for the Corvette soon referred to Dearborn's product as a "scaled-down convertible," which, in fact, it was. By contrast, the 1956 Corvette was described as a true sports car. And that, too, was accurate.

The 1956 Corvette was among the last production Chevys designed in Detroit, before GM's wholesale move to its Technical Center in Warren, Michigan, which opened in '56. The styling roots of the second-generation Corvette can be traced to two 1955 show cars, the Chevy Biscayne and the LaSalle II.

The Biscayne was a compact four-door hardtop painted light green and sporting a color-keyed interior. Its headlamps were mounted inboard, with parking lights placed in the fenders. The grille was a series of vertical bars. Air scoops were positioned at the base of the windshield, and the floor was level

1956 Corvette

with the bottom of the frame. The LaSalle II name was applied to two experimentals—one a four-door hardtop, the other (interestingly enough) a two-seat roadster. Also carefully color-keyed, both had prominent vertical-bar grilles and one particular design touch that prefigured what would later be a Corvette trademark: a concave section on the sides that swept back from the front wheel wells. This was inspired by the "LeBaron sweep" of the prewar era. The LaSalle II may have inspired some designers in Dearborn. Coincidentally, Ford stylists had come up with a similar treatment that appeared on several proposals

Vertical parking lights on Biscayne hardtop show car predicted the taillight styling of the '56 Corvette.

Another Motorama styling influence on the '56 Corvette was the LaSalle II roadster from '55.

for the 1957 Thunderbird and was considered at about the time the '56 Corvette debuted. The appearance of the "cove" panel on a competitor, of course, precluded its use on any Ford product.

Chevy offered a removable hardtop for the '56 Corvette, taken almost directly from a 1954 Motorama Corvette show car. This gave the production model—despite its new side sculpture and busy grille—a very clean look, much cleaner than either the LaSalle II or the Biscayne. Karl Ludvigsen, author of *Corvette: America's Star-Spangled Sports Car,* points out that the Mercedes-Benz 300SL gullwing coupe also influenced Chevy's thinking. The Mercedes, he said, "was responsible for the 1956 Corvette's forward-thrusting fender-lines . . . and the twin bulges in its hood panel." Corvette color choices were expanded for '56 with Onyx black, Venetian red, Cascade green, Aztec copper, Shoreline beige, and silver, in addition to the familiar Polo white.

The production model was a beautiful automobile, surely the handsomest Corvette yet. It was not garish like so many American cars of that era. It curved in all the right places for contours that looked smooth and purposeful. Its only questionable styling features were fender-mounted scoops that didn't scoop, wheel covers with dummy knock-off centers, and dashboard instruments that were more stylish than legible. But these were minor flaws in an otherwise meritorious design picture. Many afficionados believe that the '56 model and the mostly unchanged 1957 version were the most beautiful Corvettes before the Sting Ray came along in 1963.

In addition to its fine new looks, the '56 Corvette offered improvements aimed at more passenger comfort—probably a response to the five-to-one sales drubbing in '55 from the less sporty, but more luxurious Thunderbird. Among the new amenities were roll-up windows, replacing the canvas side cur-

tains of the 1953–55 model. The new hardtop offered fine visibility while providing sedan-like weather protection. Unlike the Thunderbird's porthole hardtop, the Corvette's top shunned gimmicks. Instead, its pillars were extremely thin to provide maximum all-around vision and a feeling of function—and in the sports-car market, no-nonsense design was quite the name of the game.

Under its hood, the new Corvette carried an engine derived from Ed Cole's marvelous 265 V-8 introduced the previous year. The six-cylinder models, which made up only a tiny fraction of 1955 production, were now gone for good. For the Corvette, the 265 wore a four-barrel carburetor and had 9.25:1 compression. A special high-lift cam, developed by performance engineer Zora Arkus-Duntov, raised horsepower to 225 at 5200 rpm, compared to a maximum of 205 in Chevy's family cars. Torque was 270 foot-pounds at 3600 rpm. The standard three-speed transmission and clutch combination was redesigned to handle the extra output. The clutch used 12

Lifting optional hardtop was strictly an exercise for two.

Smooth new '56 styling gave Corvette the look of a serious sports car.

heat-treated coils instead of the previous diaphragm-type spring. A 3.55:1 rear axle ratio was standard with the three-speed; a 3.27:1 ratio was optional. Powerglide automatic transmission was carried over as a $189 extra, available with the 3.55:1 gearing.

All this gave the new Corvette a level of performance that belied its civilized looks. With the manual transmission and standard rear axle ratio, the car would turn 0–60 mph in 7.5 seconds, and do the standing-start quarter mile in 16 seconds at 90-plus mph. It was capable of close to 120 mph off the showroom floor. There was some question about handling and stopping, though. The brakes were still cast-iron drums, and despite 158 square inches of lining area, they were a weak point. One road test said they "faded into oblivion" after one hard application. Handling was good—much better than Thunderbird—but understeer was still strong. Steering was quick, with just 3½ turns lock-to-lock. Weight distribution at 52/48 was nearly perfect. In all, the car showed greatly improved road behavior.

At first glance, the 1957 Corvette looked the same as the '56, but progress was evident under the skin. There was a larger V-8, a new four-speed gearbox option introduced midway through the model year, and (as Chevy boasted) up to "one horsepower per cubic inch" thanks to the new "Ramjet" fuel injection unit.

Although it had been developed by Rochester Carburetor, the Ramjet system was strictly a GM design. It incorporated a special manifold, a fuel meter, and an air meter. The air meter directed incoming air to the various intake ports, where a precise amount of fuel was squirted in to form the mixture. Fuel was delivered by a high-pressure pump driven off the distributor. The manifold was a two-piece aluminum casting. The upper part contained air passages and the metering system; the lower casting contained the ram tubes and a cover for the top of the engine.

"Fuelies" developed a rousing 283 horsepower at 6200 rpm—the first time a mass-production engine had offered one horsepower for each cubic inch of displacement. But Ramjet had its bugs. Racing set-ups had to drop the fuel cutoff during acceleration to escape flat spots. Fuel nozzles absorbed heat and caused rough idling. They were also prone to easy clogging by dirt deposits. Street users found the system hard to service. Only 240 of the 6246 Corvettes built for model year 1957 were equipped with fuel injection. But when it was healthy, the "fuelie" provided blistering performance: 0–60 mph in about 6.5 seconds was average.

The 283 cubic-inch engine was created by boring out the 265 about ⅛-inch to 3.875 inches. The 283 had higher compression, a higher-lift cam, and a choice of single (220 bhp) or dual (245 and 270 bhp) four-barrel carburetors. Fuel injection engines included a 250-bhp version as well as the 283-bhp unit, along with a third variation in racing tune. Cars with the latter came with cold-air box, 8000-rpm tachometer, and chassis modifications such as heavy-duty brakes. Ostensibly, the racing engine produced 283 bhp, too, though the figure was very likely somewhat higher.

All 283 V-8s had hydraulic valve lifters, except those with fuel injection, which used mechanical lifters. Compared to the 265, the 283 had longer-reach spark plugs, carburetor fuel filters, larger ports, wider bearings, and oil-control piston rings. Dual exhaust systems on injected versions were connected by a crossover pipe, which equalized exhaust flow through each muffler.

The final leap forward for '57 engineering was the midyear announcement of a four-speed gearbox as a $188 option. Built by Borg-Warner, it had been designed by Chevrolet engineers who started with a three-speed B-W unit, and moved reverse into the tailshaft housing to make room for a fourth forward

Styling changes for '57 were almost non-existent. The car in this "1957" factory photo is, in fact, a '56.

speed. The ratios were quite close: 2.20:1, 1.66:1, 1.31:1, and 1.00:1. The combination of the four-speed, the fuel injection engine, and the optional 4.11 rear axle ratio made the Corvette a real stormer. One test of such a car gave the following results: 0–60 mph in 5.7 seconds, 0–100 in 16.8 seconds, the standing quarter mile in 14.3 seconds at 96 mph, and a top speed of 132 mph. You'll have to guess at what it would do with a numerically lower axle ratio.

Many drivers accustomed to more exotic foreign machinery still complained about the Corvette's handling and braking. Chevy answered most of these criticisms in 1957 with RPO 684, a comprehensive suspension package. This consisted of a front anti-roll bar and heavier springing all around; larger, firmer shock absorbers; ceramic-metallic brake linings with finned, ventilated drums; "Positraction" limited-slip differential; and a quick-steering adapter that reduced turns lock-to-lock from 3.7 to 2.9. Avail-

able axle ratios ran from 3.70:1 to a super-short 4.56:1. With all the right performance hardware, a Corvette could be ready-to-race right out of the box—and race it did.

Corvette's long competition career didn't begin until the advent of the 1956–57 design. Zora Arkus-Duntov was the key. It was Duntov who had reworked the 1956 suspension for greatly improved handling. And it was Duntov who developed the cam that would yield 250 bhp and later 283. In 1956, he brought a modified Corvette with 250 bhp to Daytona Beach. That car did over 150 mph on the Florida sands. Two other Corvettes flew up to 145 and 137.

Race driver John Fitch then worked with Duntov to prepare a Corvette team for the Twelve Hours of Sebring. Three cars were built up using production versions of the record-breaking 265 engine, but fitted with two four-barrel carbs, the Duntov cam, and a ported manifold for a power output of 255. A fourth

SR-2, sans fin, at 1957 auto show

"Street" SR-2 built for Bill Mitchell

car with an engine bored out to 307 cid and fitted with a four-speed ZF transmission was entered in the prototype class. All four were equipped with Halibrand magnesium wheels, driving lights, and oversize fuel tanks. At the end of the race, Walt Hansgen and John Fitch were ninth; Ray Crawford and Max Goldman finished 15th. The prototype failed to do as well. Said Fitch: "Our performance was less than we had hoped but more than we deserved."

During the summer of 1956, Duntov built another Sebring-type car with an extended aerodynamic nose and a small tailfin on the decklid. This was Jerry Earl's famous SR-2 (also duplicated for a street machine driven by GM president Harlow Curtice). The car was campaigned extensively by Earl, Dick Thompson, and Curtis Turner. At the beginning of 1958, Jim Jeffords took over the car, painted it an ugly purple, and drove to the Sports Car Club of America (SCCA) B-production national championship. Jeffords called it the "Purple People Eater"; he might have also nicknamed it the "Purple Porsche Pulverizer." Another SR-2, a bright red car belonging to GM stylist William L. Mitchell, was also raced, but finished a mere 16th at Sebring '57.

In 1956, Dr. Richard Thompson, the Washington, D.C. dentist who became the most famous Corvette racer of the '50s, was given a C-production Corvette prepared by Duntov. This car won the C-production crown that year—the first of Thompson's championship seasons at the wheel of Corvettes. Thompson's showing was one of the turning points in the Corvette's history—it convinced Chevrolet that there was a future in building high-performance cars. This, in turn, helped Duntov justify development costs for the four-speed transmission and fuel-injected V-8 that appeared in production for '57. Those two options did more than anything else to realize the Corvette's true potential as a race car.

Starting in 1957, you could order a Corvette equipped for road racing right from the factory simply by checking off the previously mentioned RPO 684 on the options form. This provided the underpinnings for the new, enlarged, 283-cid engine with fuel injection and 283 bhp. It also moved Corvette into the B-production class. That was little handicap for the formidable Dr. Thompson: he won the

championship going away. Also that year, Thompson and Gaston Andrey took the GT class at Sebring and placed 12th overall, a happy face-saving ending after the purpose-built Sebring SS prototype failed to finish.

The Sebring SS should have been a world-beater. Duntov began work on this futuristic sports-racer in July 1956. But even with its tubular space frame, fuel injection V-8, magnesium body, and De Dion rear axle, it was an exercise in futility. The car retired after only 23 laps—run at reduced speed. The SS was really meant for Le Mans, but something happened before Duntov could get it to France: GM president Curtice announced the unexpected Automobile Manufacturers Association (AMA) decision that effectively put an end to official, direct factory support of competition. The SS program was abruptly halted and the car never raced again.

Despite these isolated disappointments on the track, Corvette rose in stature on the streets. The 1956–57 models earned respect as first-rate sports cars by the *cognoscenti* as well as the kids. One European writer noted: "Before Sebring, where we actually saw it for ourselves, the Corvette was regarded as a plastic toy. After Sebring, even the most biased were forced to admit that the Americans had one of the world's finest sports cars—as capable on the track as it was on the road. Those who drove and understood the Corvette could not help but reach that conclusion."

The only race the 1956–57 Corvette lost was the production race. Against the Thunderbird it did not do well, as these figures show:

Year	Corvette	Thunderbird
1956	3,388	15,631
1957	6,246	21,380

The Thunderbird was always intended to be a softly sprung, rather tame open two-seater, and became even more so for 1958 by growing two more seats. Meanwhile, GM had declared itself on the side of enthusiasts, regardless of the AMA's anti-racing posture. In time, the Corvette would grow in popularity to win a much larger following. By the end of the decade, it had even become a profitable item for Chevrolet Division. In the '60s, it would be impossible for anyone to imagine the Chevy lineup without it.

Zora Arkus-Duntov in the Sebring SS

Classic 1956–57 lines were spoiled by gingerbread for '58

The Great '57s: Progress and Popularity

Model year 1957 was hardly the greatest in GM history. Overall industry production was up from '56 at 7.2 million (cars and trucks), but it fell short of most estimates. Cadillac, Buick, and Oldsmobile had new designs that year. But Pontiac and Chevrolet wore third-season facelifts—and ran headlong into a striking new array of Chrysler products fresh from the drawing board of Virgil Exner, not to mention the restyled Ford and Mercury lines courtesy of George Walker. In model year production, Ford outpulled Chevy by 170,000 units; Plymouth swept back into third place ahead of Buick; Mercury and Dodge moved to within sight of Pontiac; DeSoto and Chrysler gained on Cadillac. The 1957 Chevy was accurately described by *Motor Life* magazine: "Never before has it had so much to offer. And—as a matter of fact—never has it needed it more."

Fortunately for Chevrolet, there was progress under the surface—mechanical innovations far more important than the exterior changes. At the time, this was of some help in the showrooms; today, it has left us with the most desirable postwar Chevrolet passenger car of all. The division had mated its new 283-cid V-8 with fuel injection to attain up to 283 horsepower. It had also introduced a new automatic transmission, Turboglide, engineered along the lines of Buick's Dynaflow.

Chevy's V-8 now offered a range of horsepower from 162 to 283, using both 265 and 283 cubic-inch displacements. But the hullabaloo over the new 283 overshadowed the 265, as well as the improved "Blue Flame" six. Most revisions to the six were necessitated by the new '57 styling, specifically, a lower hood line: the carburetor air cleaner was redesigned, the upper radiator tank was flatter, and the radiator water inlet was moved to the side. A genuine improvement was a fuel strainer on the inlet side of the carburetor, supplementing the fuel tank filter, to reduce the chance of flooding due to foreign material in the carb. Changes were made to the starter and generator as for the V-8s.

While clutches with higher torque capacity were used on both the 265 V-8 and the six, four-barrel and injected 283s with manual transmission had a new semi-centrifugal clutch. A new distributor was shared with the 265. There was a relocated voltage regulator and battery, and line fuses were used for lamp circuits in cars without the accessory junction block. The chassis wiring harness was divided into separate units, interconnected by multi-plugs.

Chevy's other big engineering news for '57 was Turboglide, available as an option for 283-equipped cars only. Lighter by 82 pounds than Powerglide, it utilized three turbines and two planetary gearsets in combination with a variable-pitch stator and a conventional torque converter pump. Engine power was

1957 Bel Air Nomad hardtop-wagon

1957 Bel Air convertible

1957 Bel Air convertible

sent to the driveshaft via turbine rotation through the oil in the torque converter pump. Each turbine rotated depending on the position of its vanes. As the turning force of the first turbine decreased, the second began to rotate, driving its shaft and the output shaft through the rear planetary gearset, and on to the third turbine in succession. Ultimately all three turbines freewheeled as the car gathered speed.

Turboglide offered a kickdown feature for passing, activated by flooring the accelerator. This increased the pitch on the variable-speed stator for greater torque delivery to the output shaft. The shift quadrant included a position labeled "HR" for "Hill Retarder," which helped slow the car on steep descents by creating turbulence in the oil of the torque converter to induce a drag on the rear wheels.

Rear axles and brakes were also revised for 1957. The new axle ratios were 3.36:1 for automatic, 3.55:1 for manual, and 4.11:1 for overdrive. New facing material, less sensitive to temperature changes, was applied to the front brake linings, and the front secondary brake shoe pull-back springs were increased

1957 Bel Air four-door sedan

1957 Bel Air hardtop coupe

51

1957 Two-Ten hardtop coupe

1957 Two-Ten hardtop sedan

from a 40- to 50-pound rate. Coil-type springs replaced clip-types on all brake shoes.

Though wheelbase remained 115 inches, the chassis was beefed up with new braces running from the front cross-member to the side members. Outside, overall length grew to almost 17 feet. New power control-arm ball joint and seal assemblies were used for the front suspension, and the shock absorbers were revised in line with chassis weight requirements. The rear leaf springs were moved further outboard to improve roadholding. Following an industry trend of the day, Chevy switched to 14-inch wheels and low-pressure tires, replacing the previous 15-inchers.

None of these changes were very visible, but the car itself didn't go unnoticed. The '57 styling was, in fact, a substantial facelift, and a rather successful one at that. Many of today's collectors rank it as the best-looking of the "classic Chevys."

Of course, the facelift had its limits. The big need was to make the 1955 shell last one more year; the challenge of making it look new was accepted by Styling Staff. "A three-year facelift we *had* to do," remarked former Chevrolet studio head Clare Mac-Kichan. "I guess probably that is why we did some of the things we did on the '57. We were as extreme as we could be, while saving the deck, roof, and doors. Those were the established ground rules. As I recall, there was a great deal of pressure on us in the Chev-

rolet studio [to add distinction to] the '57 car.

"We did manage to get entirely new graphics on the front, and the back was pretty different-looking, too. We did such obvious things as moving taillights to a new location, changing that whole corner. From the side we did a similar thing with the [Bel Air] aluminum panel and trim molding. We just did everything we could to change those cars, within the ground rules that we were stuck with." The effect of Exner's radical '57 Chrysler products, MacKichan concluded, was slight: "It did have an effect on what was done afterwards, in 1958 or 1959." One must remember that the '57 Chevy was in the works well before Exner's all-new designs appeared.

Though the front-end appearance was new, it didn't evolve overnight. A massive bumper surrounding a concave grille had been evident in various Chevy styling sketches dating back to 1949—even earlier if we include the 1949–50 Buick grille with its concave vertical teeth. The '57 Chevy grille can be traced back at least to 1953, when Carl Renner created a rendering surprisingly close to the design eventually used. Of this theme, Renner recalled: "Mr. MacKichan guided his men into this. We went all the way with our designs . . . and then backed off. You never can get criticized for going way out, but you always can be criticized for the lack of imagination, for not going far enough . . . Finally, when they had money to do something quite radical for Chevrolet,

1957 One-Fifty two-door utility sedan

1957 Bel Air Townsman four-door station wagon

1957 Two-Ten four-door sedan

we went into this bumper/grille.''

Attention to detail gave the '57 Chevy a lower, longer look. Compared to the 1956 model, it was 2.5 inches longer and 1.5 inches lower. A new ventilation system replaced the cowl vent, with fresh-air intake scoops located in the upper half of the headlamp bezels. Long, concealed ducts—among the car's more radical features—delivered outside air to the interior. This change allowed a lower, flatter hood, which combined with the huge bumper/grille to create an entirely new look. Twin ''lance-shaped windsplits'' substituted for the conventional hood ornament, which dated back to 1932. Tooling costs for all this were considerable, though. Stylists considered the frontal appearance heavy compared to 1955–56.

From the rear, the '57 was also quite different and, in the opinion of many, greatly improved over '56. Rear quarter panels now incorporated modest fins to accentuate the lower front end—and keep up with the competition. A panel in the molding on the trailing edge of the left rear fender swung aside to reveal the fuel filler cap.

Offering 19 body styles in the One-Fifty, Two-Ten, and Bel Air series, the 1957 Chevrolet made its debut on October 17, 1956. The only model change was replacement of a nine-passenger wagon with a six-passenger version. Numerous power team choices were available, and there were 16 solid and 15 two-

tone color combinations offered depending on series and body style.

The 283-engine cars were the fastest Chevys ever. Typically, a four-door sedan with automatic and the 270-bhp setup would do 0–60 mph in about 10 seconds and the standing quarter mile in 17.5 seconds at nearly 80 mph. No tests are available of fuel injected models, but as ''fuelie'' Corvettes would do 0–60 in 7.2 seconds, the performance of the larger passenger cars would have been a bit off that pace.

A special run of fuel injection two-doors was prepared for the Daytona Speed Weeks in early 1957, and these did rather well over a very brief racing career. In Class 4 (213 to 259 cid), Chevrolet took the first three places in the official two-way flying mile. Ford finished fourth on the Florida sands, seven seconds off the winning pace of 102.157 mph. The same day in Class 5 (259 to 305 cid) Chevrolet captured the first 33 places in a field of 37. Paul Goldsmith averaged 131.076 mph in the fastest car. Two days later, in a competition for four-barrel carburetor engines with automatic, Chevy again took 1-2-3, the best speed being Al Simonsen's 118.460. In measured-mile, standing-start acceleration runs, Chevy dominated Class 5, taking the first 18 places, the last car finishing 10 seconds ahead of the 19th-place Ford. The Manufacturer's Trophy was a Chevy sweep totaling 574 points against runner-up Ford's 309 points and third-place Mercury's 174.

Such triumphs came to a screeching halt when the Automobile Manufacturers Association (AMA) decided early in the year not to talk about—much less condone—competition. Prodded by groups like the National Safety Council, the AMA was careful to call this a ''recommendation.'' But it was effectively a racing ban, and the auto companies complied—for the first few years, anyway. As a result, racing fans were deprived of what might have been a spectacular season for the new Chevy. Incidentally, racing might have helped get the bugs out of the fuel injection system (it never happened under the AMA edict, and FI was dropped in a few years). Racing might also have speeded development of safer cars, but such reasoning has never impressed groups like the National Safety Council, which went on to help promote federal safety regulations in the '60s.

Though Chevy didn't outsell Ford for the 1957 model year, the division probably wasn't too unhappy with its volume of 1.5-plus million units. And since then, this Chevy has become recognized as one of the industry's greats. ''The design was very rare and unusual for Chevrolet,'' Carl Renner reflected. ''The people who bought Chevrolets, like myself, naturally had the feeling of wanting to own a Cad some day. Looking back, I think it was our objective to make a Chevrolet look like a 'little Cadillac.' Why *not* give people who could afford a Chevrolet that Cadillac look of quality? I thought it was a good deal. I think that is one reason why Chevrolet sold so well.''

That—and performance.

1957 Two-Ten Handyman two-door station wagon

Impala and the '58s: An Underrated First

The 1958 Chevrolet was to be all-new from the ground up. Because of this it should have been even better than the 1957 model. Why then has the '57 long since become a collector's item, while the '58 has been almost completely ignored? The reasons have rarely been explained.

Work on the 1958 design first began in June 1955 at a meeting of Chevrolet styling chief Clare Mac-Kichan, Pontiac's studio heads, and the GM body design committee. Pontiac was in on this because it would use the Chevy's new "A" body. The conclusion was that the '58s should be larger—longer, wider, and heavier—and much lower. This proved to be a key decision for Chevrolet, one that would affect other automakers, too. After all, if the top seller did something, the rest of the industry was bound to follow sooner or later. The decision to move away from the 115-inch wheelbase toward luxury-car size was significant. For better or worse, the '58 Chevy showed that even lower-priced cars could be as big as a Cadillac.

The body design was hinted at by two 1956 Motorama show cars, the Corvette-like Impala and the Biscayne. The name Impala, taken from the fleet antelope of the African plains, was intended to represent grace and speed. Compared to then-current GM production cars, both the XP-100 (the show Impala's project code) and Biscayne were more rounded, more formed. Perhaps the wildest feature on both was a compound-curve windshield, which wrapped

1958 styling preview—Biscayne show car from '55

1954 Fiat V-8 coupe by Ghia

1955 Mercedes-Benz 300SL "gullwing" coupe

1958 Impala Sport Coupe

54

1958 Impala convertible

around not only at the sides but also at the top. These show cars were mainly the creation of Chevy studio designer Jerry Cumbus, and they influenced much of the styling development for the 1958 program. But Chevrolet's glass supplier, Libby-Owens-Ford, concluded it couldn't mass produce the complex windshield curves, so that idea was shelved.

The Impala show car's front end featured the busy vertical-bar motif of the Corvette, a theme strongly desired for the '58 Chevy. Cost analysis, however, showed it couldn't be produced at a reasonable price. In the end, a sort of combination bumper/grille was adopted. This made for styling continuity with the '57 Chevy, but wasn't as distinctive as the Corvette's "teeth."

At the rear, stylists favored a dramatic approach with inwardly canted "wings" sculpted into the deck area and carrying wide, teardrop taillights. For production purposes, Chevy settled for a trio of small, round taillights on either side, rather than a complex multi-light panel. A large red teardrop did appear on the restyled 1959s with the backup lights mounted separately from it. But that car's wild fins weren't even being considered during the planning for '58. What brought them about was the appearance and popularity of Virgil Exner's "Forward Look" Chrysler products, which pushed GM out of the styling limelight in 1956–57 when the '59 Chevy was being

evolved. The 1956–60 period was probably the only time after the war that GM's styling supremacy was seriously challenged by any rival.

The shape of the 1958 Chevy owed much to European influences, too. The Mercedes-Benz 300SL "gullwing" coupe had, ironically, been replaced by a roadster by the time the Chevy arrived. But the gullwing inspired the "extractor vents" at the rear of the roof on the production Impala hardtop, as well as the grid ahead of its rear wheels. Neither of these trim bits was functional. Ghia of Turin, whose smooth Fiat coupes were also inspiring designers in the mid-'50s, contributed the prominent side-spear motif worn by all '58 Chevys.

The idea of offering a production Impala as a top-of-the-line model was suggested by the larger size of the '58s, and Chevy's determination to dominate the production race against Ford. With the Impala, Chevy entered the medium-priced field for the first time—and it hasn't left the territory since. At first, the Impala was to be quite stylistically different from the

1958 Impala Sport Coupe

1958 Bel Air Sport Sedan

other '58 models. The Chevy studio had wanted a distinctive roofline with ultra-thin pillars, lots more glass area, and a different front end from the rest of the line. But corporate cost-cutters won out, and the production Impala appeared as a mere trim option for the Bel Air hardtop coupe and convertible, available with either six or V-8 engine.

All the '58 Chevys were changed as much mechanically as they were in appearance. A new X-type frame was adopted, which allowed stylists to lower overall height without sacrificing headroom. It was some 30 percent stronger than the 1957 frame, and many observers felt it predicted the advent of unitized body/chassis construction. Because the chassis had no side rails, the body rocker panels had to be very strong. This made for considerably tighter assembly than the '57. The body and chassis were thus "integrated" to a greater degree.

Another reason for the X-member frame was that it lent itself to air suspension, "Level-Air," which

Chevy intended to offer as an option for 1958. The system, patterned after a Cadillac design, consisted of a bell-shaped rubber bellows at each wheel, and an air reserve tank mounted up front. The bellows were adjusted automatically to changes in road surface by air pressure supplied by an engine-driven compressor. Level-Air provided less nosedive and a more stable ride than the conventional suspension; ride attitude was also noticeably less affected by heavy loads in the rear. But the air suspension fad peaked almost as soon as it began, due mainly to high purchase price and reliability problems. Only a few thousand '58 Chevys were so equipped, and the option was soon canceled.

To accommodate air suspension and improve handling further, Chevy switched to trailing-arm rear suspension, with two arms per side. The lower arms were mounted to the frame, while the combined upper arms were attached to each side of the rear axle housing. Chevy called this "four link" rear suspen-

1958 Impala convertible (Script below trunklid signifies "Level-Air" suspension on this car.)

sion, and claimed it gave improved handling and shock absorber action. Up front were standard wishbones, and all four corners of conventionally suspended cars had coil springs. The result was a higher roll center, a lower center of gravity, and a softer ride with the same stability as before. The '58 was really a great step forward in suspension design.

Besides the chassis, Chevrolet tended to engines this year. The 283 was still the standard V-8, and could be had with optional fuel injection or various carburetion setups. But much interest centered around a brand-new V-8 designed from scratch—the next-generation Chevy engine. Offered with 9.5:1 compression, this 348 cubic-inch powerplant (bore and stroke 4.13×3.25) delivered up to 280 bhp at 4400 rpm. Its combustion chambers were of the cylindrical wedge shape, formed by flat-bottom heads that rested on the block faces at a 16-degree angle. Pistons were of cast aluminum, machined with 16-degree dual-sloping surfaces; lifters were oversize with hydraulic actuation. Dual exhausts were standard.

But the opposition also had new engines. Ford trotted out an enlarged 352 with over 300 bhp, and Plymouth's Golden Commando V-8 now developed up to 305 bhp. A three-way road test showed the 305 Plymouth sprinting to 60 mph in 7.7 seconds and running the standing quarter mile in 16.1. The 280-bhp Impala scored 9.1 and 16.5 seconds, respectively. Though both Plymouth and Ford got only facelifts for '58 rather than a complete restyle like Chevy, they were good-looking cars that attracted a lot of favor among press and public alike.

On the surface, Plymouth and Ford stood to lose sales in '58 among buyers who preferred a completely new look, and to gain among those interested in the best performance. Though the 348 V-8s gave Chevy better performance than in '57, the real emphasis for '58 was now on luxury, refinement, and that big-car look. Road tester Tom McCahill sensed this immediately. "If your name was Joe Zilchdrag and you wanted a heap for unwinding white-hot at Daytona Beach next February, which engine/car combination would it be?" he asked Chevrolet engineers. "As things stood when I asked the question, it was generally conceded by the boys that more performance could be wrung out of the smaller [283] engine because of valve timing and available equipment." This was an unlikely state of affairs for an engine 61 cubic inches smaller than Chevy's newest.

What saved Chevrolet in 1958 was an economic recession. The industry built only 4.25 million cars during the twelve months, against six million-plus in 1957. When the results were in, Chevy had a 30 percent slice of the market, despite being down in volume by 275,000 units. Ford, which had dropped by 700,000, slipped from a 25.6- to a 22.3-percent market share. Plymouth was off 250,000 cars, and dipped from 10.6 to 9.6 percent.

Considering this record, many observers were sur-

prised when Chevy scrapped its one-year-old '58 design for another complete restyle the following year. Actually, this was the result of a realignment in body sourcing at GM. From 1959 on, Chevy and Pontiac would share bodyshells with Buick and Oldsmobile. "The idea was to make the outer surfaces different so that nobody would know they were shared, but the thing underneath that cost the major amount of money *would* be shared," according to styling chief MacKichan. The 1958 Chevrolet was thus left in the lurch of production economics, and has been ignored by enthusiasts ever since.

It is easy to get upset about this car philosophically. Some blame if for the pernicious trend to bigger and bigger low-priced cars, for changing the traditionally nimble, middle-size package into a behemoth of little merit and distinction. Certainly the '58 Impala was directly opposite the "classic" 1955 Bel Air in concept. But viewed simply as a car, the first Impala reveals many redeeming aspects that a few collectors are now beginning to appreciate. It is highly possible that the '58 Chevy—Impalas particularly—will be one of the "comers" among desirable older cars in the 1980s.

"Many people at the time thought the design was good," remembered stylist Carl Renner. "However, there were those who referred to the rear fenders as World War I barrage balloons due to their shape and fullness. It was the first suggestion of a concave fin, leading into the larger fin in 1959. But I think it was a successful car for the time."

Certainly, the 1958 Chevy saved the sales situation in a year that bordered on disaster for the industry as a whole. It was a brand-new design—one of the few really fresh ones aside from the unlamented Edsel—in a year that needed every possible assist because of the flagging economy. This was of great importance to Chevrolet, and helped put the division in a good position for recovery in the 1960s.

The '58 Impala, whether six or V-8, is really a quite pleasant car to drive. The ride would have been called hard by the standards of 1958, but seems perfectly acceptable now. It's the kind of car that encourages long-haul motoring. There is little noise or body roll. The supple, coil-spring suspension easily copes with rough roads and sudden changes in camber. There is good road feel through the steering, a high degree of driver control. In these respects, the '58 Impala is much more likable than its clumsy, swerving, marshmallow-suspended successors of the '60s and early '70s.

Good styling, good suspension, and good performance add up to a good automobile, one that has been overlooked. Naturally, prices today are low—sometimes unbelievably so. Of all '58 Chevys, the Impala, with its luxurious interior and lush trim, is the model to look for. You can probably find a first-class hardtop or even a convertible for about what it cost new, around $2800 to $3200—maybe even less. Considering what's happened to the dollar in the 22 years since, that's a steal.

Corvair's Marvelous Monza: A Touch of Irony

As Chevy's answer to the Ford Falcon, the Corvair was a question mark. The Falcon outsold it from the time the Big Three announced their first postwar compacts in late 1959. Even Plymouth's Valiant might have outsold the Corvair, if Plymouth had the same production capacity and number of dealers as Chevy. Hasty plans for a conventional front-engine/rear-drive compact were put in motion only six months after the Corvair debuted. These matured by model year 1962 as the Chevy II, later the Nova.

But the Corvair started a trend, leading the industry to something altogether different from the bare-bones econocar. It arrived almost by accident, a last-minute addition to the Corvair line. It was just an idea from some new-forgotten marketing man for adding fractionally to Corvair sales—but it quickly became the best-selling model in the line, and kept Corvair alive through the end of the '60s. Its name, taken from the famous Italian race track, was Monza. It was first offered in 1960 as a coupe priced at only $2238.

Chevrolet's work on small, rear-engine cars began after World War II with a stillborn prototype dubbed Cadet. But in those early postwar years, buyers were so hungry for cars—even the warmed-over prewar designs that were rushed into production—that Chevy saw no real need to build anything that radical. Ford, which was toying with a small car at about the same time, concluded likewise.

By the late 1950s, however, the situation had changed dramatically. European imports, led by Volkswagen and Renault, had gained a foothold in the American market around 1955, and were taking large bites out of it by 1958. The percentage of economy-car sales was becoming too high for Detroit to ignore. Once again, U.S. automakers turned their thoughts to compacts.

One of the first, Studebaker's 1959 Lark, was so successful that it temporarily halted its maker's ultimate demise. A year earlier, American Motors had resurrected its 100-inch-wheelbase Rambler from 1955 and called it the American. At that time, GM had pinned its hopes on "captive" imports made by its overseas subsidiaries. The Opel Kadett from Germany and the Vauxhall Victor from England were sold for awhile, but they weren't enough. Besides, many buyers distrusted funny little "furrin" cars. So, the Big Three launched compact-car development programs almost at the same time. The results were the Valiant, Falcon, and Corvair, all of which bowed for the 1960 model year.

The Corvair was largely conceived and planned by long-time GM engineer Edward N. Cole, father of the postwar Cadillac and Chevy V-8s, director of Chevy engineering, later Chevy general manager, and still later, GM president. Cole always liked the Corvair, even after its unfortunate bout with publicity-seeking

1960 Corvair 700 four-door sedan

1958 clay for Corvair two-door based on 1960 sedan

1967 Corvair Monza hardtop sedan

muckrakers. To the day he died, he proclaimed his love for it, and it was easy to see why. It was an engineer's car through and through.

By far the most radical of the Big Three compacts, the Corvair shunned the conventional water-cooled engine mounted up front for an air-cooled, rear-mounted "pancake six." Initially, it displaced 140 cubic inches (bore and stroke of 3.38 × 2.60) and developed 80 bhp in standard tune; 95 bhp was available as an option. Relatively complicated, the design featured two cylinder heads and six separate cylinder barrels, plus a divided crankcase. Production

engines weighed close to 400 pounds each, about 100 pounds more than Cole had planned. And this miscalculation would prove to have a negative effect on the car's handling.

The suspension of the 108-inch wheelbase Corvair was possibly too basic for such a pioneering design. At the front were wishbones and coil springs; at the rear were semi-trailing swing axles. There was no anti-sway bar at either end, although GM was well aware of how to use this device to minimize the oversteer in hard cornering inherent in a rear-engine car. Management's decision to hold down production

Factory photo identifies this prototype as the "Corvair 900 2 DR Sedan"

PINKY RANDALL

59

costs while maximizing ease of service and efficiency of assembly prevented the use of more sophisticated geometry until 1962. That year, a regular production option was added consisting of stiffer springs, shorter rear axle limit straps, and a front anti-sway bar. A major suspension improvement occurred in 1964 when a rear transverse compensating spring was adopted. The suspension of the completely reworked 1965 Corvair bore no resemblance to the 1960 setup. Unfortunately, all these changes came much too late.

There's a sense of irony about public reaction to this novel, efficient, economical car. Consumer advocates, who today preach the virtues of small cars, should have welcomed the Corvair. Instead, they panned it. This is not to say that Ralph Nader's book, *Unsafe at Any Speed,* killed the Corvair all by itself—even though Nader likes to take credit for that. Economics also played a part. After the initial sales battle was lost to Falcon, Corvair depended on the sporty Monza for its survival. But the Monza was a success mainly because it was virtually alone in the sporty compact field—indeed, it created the market. Once Ford brought out the Mustang, however, Monza sales began to decline as Chevrolet was forced to react to, rather than anticipate, its chief rival. Six months before Nader's book was published, the word had gone out to let the Corvair fade away quietly. In a GM directive dated April 1965 it was stated: "No more development work. Do just enough to keep it up with the safety standards." (Safety standards had been multiplying since the industry's voluntary adoption of amber parking lights in 1962; seatbelts were already required by 1965.)

It should be understood, though, that the rather simple all-independent suspension of the 1960–63 Corvair did not create a dangerous or ill-handling car, as various lawsuits (encouraged by the Nader book) alleged. To be sure, the car *did* oversteer—but most rear-engine cars do. The oversteer was not excessive if tire pressures were maintained at the levels recommended in the owner's manual: 15 psi front, 26 psi rear. The problem was that many drivers didn't pay much attention to tire pressures, and they were critical on the Corvair. The car wasn't cleared until a Congressional investigation found in its favor, years after it was discontinued.

Back to the Monza. It's surprising how little it really differed from other Corvair models. Its main attraction was a snazzy, color-keyed interior with front bucket seats—something of a first for a budget-priced domestic car. The rear seat was a bench that folded down to provide extra luggage space, and was upholstered in a way that suggested buckets. Deep-pile carpeting came as standard, as did a deluxe steering wheel, cigarette lighter, special armrests, and more attractive window hardware. On the outside, bright metal around the window frames and "Monza 900" emblems were the main identifying marks. The Monza was announced late in the 1960 model year so only 11,926 were built, but this doesn't

1962 Corvair Monza coupe

begin to reveal how important it was. In 1961, with the addition of a four-door version, Monza accounted for 143,000 of Corvair's 330,000 sales. In 1962, two out of every three Corvairs sold were Monzas.

The Monza was improved with each passing year, of course, and this certainly helped sales. For 1961, for example, the engine was bored out to 145 cubic inches for 95 bhp standard or 98 bhp optional. In 1964, a stroke increase brought a displacement to 164 cubic inches (3.44×2.95), and output rose to 110 bhp with the standard carburetor setup. The addition of a convertible for 1962 gave Monza more sports-car appeal than ever. Keeping up with a properly optioned, well-driven Monza on a bit of winding road was not always an easy chore for Triumph or MG drivers—much to their embarrassment.

A key feature in the Monza's success story was its optional four-speed all-synchromesh manual transmission with floor-mounted shifter, introduced on the 1961s. This greatly improved flexibility, especially in traffic. The gear ratios, though, could have been better chosen. "It is just possible to start out in 2nd gear," *Motor Trend* magazine reported, "indicating that 1st and 2nd are very close together while 3rd is too high up the scale. A very unscientific but reliable seat-of-the-pants feel during acceleration bears this out. Second gear pushes the driver right back in

John Fitch and the Fitch Sprint in 1962

1963 Corvair Monza convertible

1969 Corvair Monza coupe

the seat while 3rd seems to die in comparison ... Ratios chosen purely for even acceleration would be more nearly equal." In later models, Chevrolet solved this problem by providing better-spaced gears and a wider choice of final drive ratios.

Most testers felt that the degree of final oversteer exhibited by pre-1964 Monzas was acceptable on the grounds that the typical owner would never press the car that hard. This proved to be wishful thinking, as later lawsuits bore out. But in fact, for the vast majority of owners, the Corvair never seemed to lose its head. "Moving through traffic is a pleasure," stated one road test of a '61. "There is plenty of power on tap, and it is possible to slip through spaces that are prohibitive for full-sized machinery. Parking is a breeze and feels almost like power steering. At high speeds on the open road the Monza tracks nicely, isn't adversely affected by crosswinds or road crown." The tester summed up by saying "[The Monza] is certainly an excellent compromise choice for the family man/enthusiast who wants low-cost sports motoring. In fact, it is a temptation to call it the Poor Man's Porsche."

Proof of this flattering assessment was soon available in the form of that now-legendary Monza offshoot, the Fitch Sprint. Built by racing driver John Fitch, who had unlimited faith in the Corvair design, the Sprint was perhaps the closest any Chevrolet

had ever come to the European idea of grand touring. Fitch's performance, handling, and appearance alterations turned the already attractive Monza coupe into a truly outstanding road car.

The Fitch engine kit, selling for just $29 installed, raised output of the flat six to 155 bhp, good for 0–60 mph times of around 9.5 seconds. Other modifications were available for the suspension. Pre-1965 Sprints were distinguished by a vinyl-topped roof, racing stripes, and chrome-plated stone guards for the headlamps. Fitch gradually expanded his line of accessories and mechanical options, adding a quick-steering kit, a racing-type steering wheel, various road wheels, and the like. Because they are rare today, Sprints are among the most highly-prized of Corvairs.

The most popular production Corvair by a country mile, the Monza lived through the total restyle of 1965, on to the last of the line in 1969—always sporty, always attractive, always a car to be driven rather than simply steered. It was—and occasionally still is—raced successfully in sedan classes. It even inspired Europe's great *carrozzeria* to create exotic gran turismo designs around its mechanical components. Despite its commercial significance, however, the Monza was not the ultimate Corvair. That title belongs to the 1962–64 Monza Spyder and the 1965–66 Corsa.

1967 Corvair Monza hardtop sedan

Last of the line—the 1969 Corvair

Sting Ray: The Classic Corvette

Although the Corvette received many important changes during its first 10 years of production, none of them really changed the design very much. The X-braced frame and basic fiberglass body panels were unaltered except in detail from 1953 through 1962. But the 1963 Sting Ray was a complete revision, except that it retained the '62 engine lineup. In addition to the roadster, there was also a beautiful grand touring coupe. Each sold over 10,000 copies, putting Corvette production over 21,000 for the model year—about 50 percent better than any previous season. As the first of an entirely new line of Corvettes, the '63 has since received just recognition as a landmark design.

The overriding goal for the '63 model, according to Zora Arkus-Duntov, was "better driver and passenger accommodation, better luggage space, better ride, better handling, and higher performance." Styling Staff's first answer to these requisites originated in late 1959 as project XP-720. Based on the Stingray* racer, this coupe had a smooth fastback fuselage set off by a distinctive split rear window. The divided backlight was Bill Mitchell's idea, and

he'd had a rough time selling it to the practical Duntov. It made production, but only for 1963. As far as Mitchell was concerned, subsequent models with the one-piece backlight lacked a certain character. "If you take that [the divider bar] off," he said, "you might as well forget the whole thing."

The rest of Mitchell's 1963 Sting Ray package was practical as well as attractive. Early alterations to the Stingray racer included hidden headlights, with the lamp units mounted in pivoting sections that fit flush with the cleanly creased front end. Styling Staff created an attractive dip in the beltline at the upper trailing edge of the door, and the coupe's doors were cut into the roof, like the '48 Tucker. Speaking of influential predecessors, the name DeSoto comes up twice. The 1942 DeSoto was the last previous car with hidden headlights. And the 1955–56 DeSoto had a dash with a "gullwing" shape, the essential element in the Corvette's cockpit. "The dual cockpit was widely criticized at the time," one Corvette designer remembers. "But it was a very fresh approach to two-passenger styling, and I think it worked remarkably well."

1963 Corvette Sting Ray "split-window" coupe

'63 Sting Ray roadsters with (top) and without optional hardtop

With the XP-720 coupe firmed up, other body styles were created, including a roadster version. Ed Cole had wanted a four-seater too, but both Mitchell and Duntov opposed this, saying the Corvette's distinction lay in its uncompromising two-seat configuration. A 2+2 coupe (later tried with dubious aesthetic success by sometime-rival Jaguar) was also considered but never developed.

The finished coupe and roadster styling was subjected to intensive evaluation, including wind tunnel

Between 1963 and 1967, the name was carried as two words. The previous racing car and post-1968 models used a one word spelling.

tests at Cal Tech. Body engineers spent a lot of time adding and subtracting weight. Compared to the 1962 Corvette, the Sting Ray had almost twice as much steel support built into its central body structure. But this was balanced by a reduction in fiberglass to make its body slightly lighter than the '62.

The new design was planned around a shorter, 98-inch wheelbase, and rear track was two inches narrower. Frontal area was reduced by one square foot. Yet interior space was at least as good as before in every direction. And, thanks to the added steel reinforcement, the cockpit was stronger and safer.

Other body features included curved side windows, cowl-top ventilation, more luggage space, and a much improved fresh-air heater. But there was no

Sting Ray for 1963—first of the timeless fourth-generation Corvettes

external decklid. You had to reach in behind the seats to get to the trunk space. The spare tire was placed in a special hinged housing, which dropped to ground level for access.

Although engines stayed the same, the chassis was changed—primarily at the rear. The new, fully independent rear suspension was a three-link type with double-jointed open driveshafts on each side, control arms, and trailing radius rods. A single transverse leaf spring (there was no room for coils) was

mounted to the frame with rubber-cushioned struts. In accordance with Duntov's wishes, the differential was also bolted to the rear cross-member, insulated with rubber at the mounting points. The frame itself was a well-reinforced box. Weight distribution was rearranged to 48/52, instead of the previous 53/47. Ride and handling were significantly better as a result, and axle tramp was reduced. A new recirculating-ball steering gear combined with a dual-arm, three-link, ball-joint front suspension to provide

Rear window divider vanished on the '64 coupe.

1963's fake hood vents were erased for the '64 Sting Ray.

Different roof vents, wheel covers, and a one-piece rear window distinguish the '64 Sting Ray coupe.

Vertical front fender louvers appeared for '65. Car shown has fuel injection, which was in its final year.

fewer turns lock-to-lock than before. The front brake drums were wider, and all brakes were of the self-adjusting type. Contemporary engineering practice dictated an alternator instead of a generator, positive crankcase ventilation, a smaller flywheel, and a new aluminum clutch housing.

Competition options for the coupe were extensive, suggesting GM's intent that it become a GT-class and SCCA contender. They included heavy-duty springs and shocks, stiffer anti-sway bar, metallic brake linings, Al-Fin aluminum brake drums, cast-aluminum knock-off wheels, dual master cylinder, and a 36.5-gallon fuel tank. Full leather upholstery was also available.

Road testers raved about the new Sting Ray, especially liking its greatly improved traction. It neither hopped during hard acceleration nor oversteered on tight bends. Testing a coupe on a series of S-turns, *Road & Track* magazine said: "Every time through it we discovered we could have gone a little faster."

1966 Sting Ray coupe got new eggcrate grille, and restyled rocker panels and wheelcovers. Note absence of roof vents.

Mark IV engine was bored out to 427 cid for 1966, came with special "power bulge" hood.

1967 Sting Ray coupe got revised front fender vents, clean rockers. Wheel trims signify this car's all-disc braking system.

The excitement generated by the Sting Ray in the early and mid-'60s resulted from its continual improvement year after year. Contrary to the old Detroit habit of adding trim and meaningless medallions, GM actually removed the stuff from subsequent models. In 1964, the controversial split rear window disappeared, slotted wheel discs were added, and the fake hood louvers were erased. The coupe's rear quarter vents were redesigned and made partly functional as air extractors for the ventilation system. In 1965, the hood panel was completely smoothed off, and the front fender slots were opened up to serve as heat ducts for the engine compartment. The coupe's inefficient extractor vents were deleted altogether in 1966, when an egg-crate grille was also adopted. By 1967, the car was

nearly perfect. The only styling changes were a central oblong backup light, revised front fender louvers, bolt-on instead of knock-off aluminum wheels, and an optional black vinyl covering for the roadster's removable hardtop.

Mechanically, however, each of the Sting Ray years brought important advancements. The new fuel-injected 375-bhp small-block engine for 1963 developed 1.15 bhp per cubic inch. With it, the Corvette could leap from 0 to 100 mph in just 15 seconds. For 1965, disc brakes appeared on all four wheels—something the car buffs had been demanding for years. In 1965, too, came another big surprise: the Mark IV V-8 with 425 hp.

Big-engined 'Vettes had been built earlier. Mickey Thompson's specials with the 409 for Daytona and

Few appearance changes marked the '67 Sting Ray. 1963–67 design was the shortest-lived of all Corvettes.

At home on any road, the '67 Sting Coupe tackles a twisty mountain trail.

other races had been seen as early as 1962. Zora Duntov had first resisted the idea of a big-block production Corvette, but by '64 the need was obvious. Cars like the AC Cobra were wowing enthusiasts, and beginning to trounce Corvettes soundly on the race tracks. Duntov teamed with Jim Premo, who had replaced Harry Barr as Chevrolet chief engineer, to work out the adaptation.

Initially, the engine was a 396-cid unit (4.09 × 3.76 inches), since GM policy restricted anything smaller than an intermediate to less than 400 cubic inches. (It replaced the 365-bhp small-block Corvette option.) With 11:1 compression, four-barrel carburetor, and solid lifters, it belted out 425 bhp at 6400 rpm, accompanied by 415 foot-pounds of torque at 4000 rpm. To handle such brute force, there were stiffer front springs, a thicker front sway bar, new rear sway bar, heavier clutch, and a larger radiator and fan. Though the Mark IV weighed over 650 pounds, the car's weight distribution remained near neutral at 51/49. An aggressive-looking hood bulge and optional side-mounted exhaust pipes completed a very impressive package.

For 1966, a bore increase to 4.25 inches gave 427 cid—and truly astounding acceleration. With the 4.11:1 rear axle ratio, a car tested by *Sports Car Graphic* magazine managed 0–60 mph in a nearly unbelievable 4.8 seconds, 0–100 in 11.2, and a flat-out maximum of 140 mph. The only thing that could touch it was a 427 Cobra—more of an out-and-out competition car, with none of the high-speed comfort qualities of the Sting Ray. The big-inch 'Vette was truly in a class by itself.

Other changes at the lower end of the performance scale during the Sting Ray years bear mentioning. Fuel injection was dropped after 1965, mainly due to its high production costs, low sales, and the advent of the Mark IV program. Engine options may be summarized as follows:

Years	CID	Induction	bhp/rpm
63–65	327	carburetor	250/4400
63–67	327	carburetor	300/5000
63	327	carburetor	340/6000
65–67	327	carburetor	350/5800
63	327	injection	360/6000
64–65	327	injection	395/6200
65	396	carburetor	425/6400
66–67	427	carburetor	390/5400
66	427	carburetor	425/6400
67	427	carburetor	400/5400
67	427	carburetor	435/5800

By the time Elliot M. "Pete" Estes (today GM president) had relieved Semon E. "Bunkie" Knudsen as Chevrolet general manager in 1965, the Corvette was permanently established in the divisional picture. No longer did anyone question its value—not with sales of over 20,000 units annually. Production figures for each Sting Ray model year are as follows:

Year	Coupe	Conv	Total
1963	10,594	10,919	21,513
1964	8,304	13,925	22,229
1965	8,186	15,376	23,562
1966	9,958	17,762	27,720
1967	8,504	14,436	22,940

But Bill Mitchell and Styling Staff were now ready with a successor. The 1963–67 Sting Ray is thus the shortest-lived Corvette design of all. This should not belie the fact that it may have been the ultimate expression of the sports car as visualized by Mitchell, Zora Arkus-Duntov, Ed Cole, and other GM personalities who were car *lovers* as well as car builders. Altogether, nearly 120,000 copies were sold. Today, these are among the most sought-after Corvettes of all. They brought the Corvette to its pinnacle of development—beautifully engineered, gracefully proportioned.

Super Sports: They Put the Fun Back

The early '60s saw the gradual emergence of slow-turning, big-block V-8s with tremendous torque and horsepower. Chevy's contribution to this trend was the well-remembered 409. Originally designed for stock-car and drag racing, the ultimate version of this engine (1963) had a hot cam and dual

1961 Impala Super Sport hardtop coupe

1962 Impala Super Sport convertible

four-barrel carburetors for 425 bhp with 425 foot-pounds of torque. Chevy dropped out of stock-car racing (officially) in 1962 for the second time since the AMA ruling of 1957. But 409s were the cars to beat on the drag strips that year, and one took the Stock Eliminator trophy in the National Hot Rod Association (NHRA) championships.

While street versions of the "SS" 409 weren't usually sold in the top state of tune, they had more than enough muscle to transform the "soft" image of Chevrolet's big cars. Equipped with bucket seats, four-speed gearbox, handling options, and sintered metallic brake linings, the SS Chevy was among the world's fastest cars over all kinds of roads, straight and twisty. The SS was initially a package of various options ostensibly available on any full-size body style in 1961–63; for 1964–67 there was a separate Impala SS series consisting of a two-door hardtop and convertible. It's no exaggeration to say these mighty Chevys put back the fun in big-car driving.

An indication of just how potent an SS could be was provided by *Car Life* magazine, which tested a specially modified 1963 SS 409 owned by drag racer Frank Sanders of Phoenix, Arizona. Sanders started with the basic 409-bhp engine (bore and stroke 4.31 × 3.50). He used Jahns pistons, but retained the stock rods, crankshaft, and valve gear. Reciprocating parts were balanced, and bearing surfaces were micro-finished. Fine tuning, including richer carburetor main jets, a 22-degree BTDC spark advance, and cold plugs, added up to something over 430 bhp.

Sanders' car used standard Chevy RPOs (Regular Production Options) to round out the package. These included a Warner Gear four-speed all-synchromesh transmission with 2.20:1 first gear, 4.56:1 Positraction differential, heavy-duty suspension, and steering-column-mounted electric tach. The car started life as a Bel Air hardtop, which was slightly lighter than the corresponding Impala version.

The results of all this were, predictably, impressive. Sanders' car actually turned a 12.22-second, 115-mph quarter-mile elapsed time in its first race. The 0–60 mph dash took just four seconds flat. The

1961 Impala Super Sport hardtop coupe

shift from third to fourth was made at 6500 rpm and 88 miles an hour.

The remarkable thing about the SS was its extreme flexibility. "We won't attempt to evaluate this particular car as a street vehicle," noted *Car Life,* "since it is tuned and rebuilt with the quarter-mile drag strip in mind. However, Sanders' wife drives it daily to and from Arizona State University classes. It truly can be called a dual-purpose car. Note, too, that a 409 can be set up as a fine high-speed highway tourer; all it requires is Chevrolet's optional heavy-duty suspension and sintered metallic brakes. And if the same thoughtful approach used by Sanders and others for drag racing were applied to this purpose, it would probably result in a 150-mph *Gran Turismo!"*

A more docile, slightly detuned version of the SS was offered with 380 bhp for 1962 and 340 for 1963. Interestingly, the 340 turned out 420 foot-pounds of torque at 3200 rpm—only five less than the racing engine, and at 1000 rpm lower on the rev scale. In other words, the 380/340 was almost as fast at midrange speeds, and was more practical for all-around driving. A well-tuned example could return 0–60 mph times of under 8 seconds.

You can hardly talk about the 1961–63 SS Chevys without mentioning their fine styling. After the nightmare of 1959, Chevy design recovered rapidly. For 1960, the weird bat fins were cropped, and then completely disappeared on the rebodied '61 model. The facelifted 1962 edition was ultra-clean. For 1963, there was yet another new bodyshell with more sculptured lines that were light years away from the

1962 Impala Super Sport hardtop coupe

1963 Impala Super Sport hardtop coupe

69

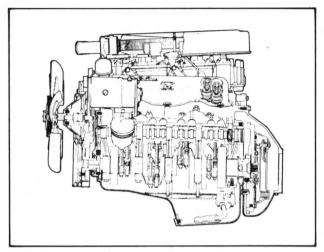

The trend-setting "409" V-8—heart of the SS

1964 Impala Super Sport hardtop coupe

outlandish '59. Most SS 409s were, of course, Impalas. They were fitted with comfy twin bucket seats up front, separated by a slim center console containing an auxiliary glovebox and the shift lever. A minor problem was lack of nighttime illumination for the shift quadrant on cars with automatic, which made range selection a matter of groping in the dark. But people who were serious about SS performance usually specified the four-speed manual anyway.

Of course, the SS was not without its faults, although objectively speaking, they were common to most big cars of the day. Its steering was too slow and low-geared, really, even with power assist, for a car with so much brute strength. The standard suspension gave a ride that was far too soft, and no SS was worth its salt without the GM handling package

(heavy-duty springs and shocks). Metallic brake linings were virtually mandatory. With 3500 to 4000 pounds of mass to contend with, the standard brakes would not survive more than two panic stops in quick succession from 80 or 90 mph. Several testers criticized the "bathtub" feel created by the low driving position, suggesting that the seats should have been higher off the floor and the steering wheel closer to the dash, or at least adjustable. "But, while we criticize some of the minor things about the car, we can enthuse about its general concept," wrote *Car Life*.

In 1964, the SS became a separate series in the Chevrolet lineup for the first time. Sitting above the standard Impala, it was offered in four permutations, a two-door hardtop and a convertible with either six or V-8 power. (The six-cylinder SS was a contradic-

1965 Impala Super Sport convertible

tion in terms, and few were built—never more than 500 a year.) The exterior featured special emblems, but was minus the regular Impala's rocker panel brightwork. Vinyl bucket seats and a center console were standard, while a tachometer and "sport" steering wheel were optional. All the usual performance goodies were still listed, including the 380/409-bhp 409 V-8, handling package, sintered metallic brake linings, and four-speed manual gearbox. A quick-ratio power steering option, introduced for '64, cured the excess wheel twirling of previous models. Liberal use of the option book could, of course, raise the price of an SS considerably. Still, it is nostalgic to wander through the price sheets and note, for example, that only $2947 put you in a V-8 hardtop in 1964 and $3196 bought a convertible.

For 1965, the 409 lost some of its punch as Chevy dropped the dual four-barrel carburetor setup. Maximum available horsepower was now 400 by means of a single four-barrel carb mounted on a large-port aluminum manifold, plus solid-lifter cam, streamlined cast-iron exhaust manifolds, and an 11:1 compression ratio. "It's plenty strong for the street in the Chevy big cars," noted *Motor Trend* magazine, "but no longer competitive in the Super/Stock or A/S classes on the drag strip." Also available was the 340-bhp 409 with 10:1 compression, single four-barrel carburetor, and a moderately hot hydraulic-lifter camshaft.

A midyear entry for the '65 season was Chevy's new Mark IV 396-cid V-8, which eventually replaced the 409. This great performance powerplant was descended from the fabulous Mark II 427 (said to have developed over 550 horsepower) built for the Daytona Speed Weeks in February 1963. The 396 was

1966 Impala Super Sport convertible

close to the Mark II in concept, but had a stronger bottom end for long-term reliability.

The Mark IV's key engineering feature was its "porcupine" cylinder head, so-called because of the varying tilt of its valves. (They were situated in opposite directions laterally and longitudinally, and were staggered along the length of the head, instead of lined up in a row.) The aim of this configuration was breathing similar to that of a hemi-head engine, but without its high manufacturing costs. A secondary purpose was to eliminate the need for double rocker shafts and exhaust rocker arms typical of a hemi.

Technical writer Roger Huntington observed: "Chevrolet may have compromised slightly on breathing, but not much. The valve tilt across the head allows short ports with a minimum of curvature.

1967 Impala Super Sport convertible

This is the big secret of the hemi head. But Chevrolet has had to do more—because their valves were staggered along the length of the head, and there would still be shrouding around the outside edges by the chamber walls. They got around this by tilting the valves *inward* toward the center of the cylinder (as viewed from the side). This let the valves open away from the walls, for minimum shroud restriction. Result: near hemi-head breathing with a very simple valve layout . . . They say the new 396 has 'breathing and rpm potential' to 8000 revs.''

The Mark IV 396 was offered for the Corvette, Chevelle, and full-size Chevrolet lines, including the new Caprice (arriving in mid-1965 as a trim option for Impala four-door hardtops and expanded into a separate series for 1966). There were 325- and 425-bhp versions. The former had 10:1 compression, hydraulic cam, moderate valving and porting, a single four-barrel Rochester carburetor, and single exhaust. The 425 had 11:1 compression, a hot solid-lifter cam, enormous ports and valves, a large Holley four-barrel carburetor, big-port aluminum manifold, cast-iron streamlined headers, and dual exhausts. Both engines were initially available with Turbo Hydra-Matic or three-speed, all-synchro heavy-duty manual transmission. With 410 or more foot-pounds of torque, there was little reason for a four-speed, although one was later added to the option list anyway. As installed, the 396 gave the Impala SS exhilarating performance, with 0–60 mph times of around 8 seconds for the mild version, and less for the 425.

For 1967, the last year for the Impala SS, the Mark IV engine was bored out to 427 cid, but horsepower dropped to 385. (The only reason it hadn't been over 400 cid before was that Chevrolet policy prohibited such engines from intermediates. The 396 SS Chevelle was thus continued for 1967.) As in previous years, there ostensibly *were* six-cylinder SS models for sale, but only about 400 were built. The rest of the 74,000 Impala SS cars that year were V-8s, and about 9500 were convertibles. The usual three transmissions were offered: three- and four-speed manuals, plus Turbo Hydra-Matic. Most testers preferred the latter, suggesting that it provided an ideal compromise for both city and highway driving. Disc brakes were a new option that year, and highly recommended. Also featured were a dual-circuit brake system with a dashboard brake failure warning light, a collapsible steering column, and door locks that had to be released before the inside handles worked. The '67 SS used Wide-Oval tires, which improved high-speed stability and stopping power.

In design, the Impala (both regular and SS versions) was remarkably consistent throughout the '60s. It retained a 119-inch wheelbase for the entire decade, even though Chevy abandoned the X-type frame for a full-perimeter chassis in 1965. Styling changes were evolutionary. The new bodyshell for '65 brought flowing lines and a slight upward sweep to the rear quarter panels, a shape that continued right on through 1968, after which more bulging body contours were adopted. Certainly the mid-decade cars were the prettiest, the 1962-64s in particular.

The only thing that prevents the SS from being even more desirable as a collector's item is the higher price and lower octane ratings of today's gasoline. The octane problem can be solved by additives, and many collectors are willing to restrict their driving a little in order to enjoy an SS. Even so, these cars were all built before engine-choking emissions devices became mandatory, which means that they can return quite reasonable gas mileage when driven conservatively. Only the hairy 400-plus-bhp models are extremely thirsty.

So if the spirit moves you, you may want to check out the next clean, original SS that comes your way. The SS was a great tribute to Chevrolet. It proved that big cars didn't have to be dull, slow, or spongy. It was the essence of what driving was all about in the high-revving '60s.

Swan song for the SS—the '67 Impala Super Sport convertible

Great Cars From Chevrolet

COLOR SHOWCASE II

1957 Bel Air convertible

Above: 1957 Two-Ten Sport Coupe

Below: 1957 Bel Air convertible

1957 Bel Air Nomad hardtop wagon

Above: 1963 Corvette Sting Ray "split-window" coupe

Below: 1964 Corvair Monza Spyder coupe

1964 Corvair Monza Spyder convertible

Above: 1966 Impala Super Sport convertible

Below: 1965 Corvair Monza convertible

Above: 1969 Camaro Z-28 sport coupe

Below: 1969 Camaro sport coupe

Above: 1969 Roger Penske Camaro Z-28, driven by Mark Donohue, in Trans-Am action

Below: 1970½ Camaro Rally Sport coupe

GM PHOTOGRAPHIC

Spyder and Corsa: The Ultimate Corvairs

The Corvair Monza, with its bucket-seat interior, four-speed gearbox, and bright styling, started the whole sporty compact phenomenon in the '60s. Its concept was soon copied for other compacts, and had even spread to intermediate and full-size cars by mid-decade. In this respect, the Monza was a milestone.

But despite its unique and winning personality, the Monza was no powerhouse, and was usually embarrassed at the inevitable, informal stop-light drag race. More "oomph" was clearly needed. Chevy responded with the Monza Spyder of 1962–64, and its successor, the Corsa of 1965–66. In many ways, they were just as significant as the original Monza, and there can be little argument that they were the ultimate Corvairs.

"From the top of the famous turbocharger, overlooking the air-cooled engine room, we bring you the exhaustive music of the Corvair Monza Spyder and the flat six." Unconventional advertising was not unusual in the '60s, except that in this case, staid old family-toting Chevy was doing the tooting. The bally-

hoo was about the turbocharger, which had never been seen previously on American production cars. Along with its air-cooled rear engine and four-wheel independent suspension (shared with lesser Corvairs), the turbocharged Monza Spyder was a significant contribution to postwar automotive development.

Blowers of different types had been tried on Corvairs before. Andy Granatelli's Paxton Products, for example, had developed their SN-60 centrifugal model as a $365 performance item. On Granatelli's own '60 Corvair coupe, this belt-driven device cut the 0–60 mph time from 13.5 to 7.8 seconds and provided 142 mph flat out at Bonneville. Chevrolet itself had fitted a Paxton supercharger to its Corvair "Sebring Spyder SS" show car of 1961, and did quite a lot of experimenting with it. But the Paxton blower sapped power because it was always in operation, and was only mildly effective at low speeds. GM thus turned to turbocharging.

The turbo-supercharger or turbocharger was invented in the early '20s, initially for aircraft engines.

Convertible was new Corvair body style for '62. Monza Spyder version was the rarest.

It was later adapted for diesel truck installations where it is now virtually universal. Corvair engineers recognized that turbocharging (as opposed to pure supercharging) had several obvious advantages: no mechanical drive, less noise and vibration, more efficient space utilization, on-demand functioning, a very slight drop in overall fuel economy, increased power, and lower cost. Accordingly, engineers J. O. Brafford and R. E. Threson were assigned responsibility for developing a production turbo-super-charged engine suitable for the Corvair.

Turbocharging works much like a windmill driven by moving air. In this case, the "wind" is exhaust gas, which spins a turbine wheel called an impeller. Power is transferred by a shaft connected to another impeller (compressor) that squeezes (pressurizes) fuel and air into a very dense mixture. As the rate of exhaust flow increases and the temperature rises,

the compressor turbine spins faster and faster, creating positive pressure or "boost" in the manifold.

The Corvair Spyder's turbocharger, manufactured by Thompson Valve Division of Thompson-Ramo-Wooldridge Inc., had an 11-blade exhaust impeller made of heat-resistent, cobalt-base alloy. It was cast integrally with a 1/2-inch-diameter shaft in a snail-shaped housing. Exhaust gases flowed inward from the outer edge of the housing and exited at the side. A die-cast, aluminum-alloy, 14-blade compressor was bolted to the other end of the exhaust impeller shaft. This pressurized the fuel/air mixture outwards from the center, where it had entered. The complete unit weighed only 13.5 pounds. It was mounted toward the forward part of the engine compartment, four inches off center, to leave space for heater ducting. A third aluminum housing separated the two components, and contained a floating bearing for the shaft. In airplanes, turbochargers are often mounted close to the cylinders. This was impractical on the Corvair, so the unit was connected to a chromed crossover pipe that bolted directly to the cylinder heads in place of the carbs. Exhaust flow through the engine's stock twin manifolds was routed through a lower crossover pipe mounted ahead of the engine, then up and into the turbine chamber. The gas exited to the right of the casting, and flowed through a pipe to the muffler. A cast-iron heat shield protected the bearing housing and compressor end of the turbo.

A conventional Carter YH sidedraft carb was selected for the turbo engine (the same carb used with different jets on six-cylinder Corvettes and the Nash-Healey Le Mans cars). It had three concentric venturis, and was dressed up with chrome bolt heads and linkages, set against a glossy, black-finished carburetor body.

During initial testing, turbochargers caused chronic parts failures on stock Corvair engines, so super-strength materials were specified for many internal components—chrome steel for the crankshaft,

1963 Corvair Monza Spyder convertible

1964 Corvair Monza Spyder convertible

DAVID NEWELL

ibles of all kinds were hard to come by in 1962, the first year for that happy body style.

There was more to the Monza Spyder than its intriguing engine and standard heavy-duty suspension. Chrome abounded in the engine room: crossover pipe, oil lines, fuel lines, dipstick handle, and exhaust shield. These were set off against matte-black shrouding designed to protect the spare tire, mounted in the engine compartment, from the turbo's heat. On the outside, a 2.5-inch chrome tailpipe protruded from a special outlet in the body, lending the Spyder a more authoritative look than other Corvairs. A die-cast emblem with special logo was attached to the rear deck, and 13 different colors were available. One more color was added for 1963-64, but no Spyders were ever two-toned.

Entering the Spyder's cockpit, the driver encountered a businesslike instrument display—6000-rpm tach, 120-mph speedometer, and fuel, manifold pressure, and temperature gauges—with a brushed-aluminum appliqué. In the center was a brushed-aluminum radio panel, and the same material covered the glovebox door in front of the passenger.

For 1963, Spyder production was up despite a 12.7 percent drop in total Corvair sales. Of course, Chevrolet was partly trying to catch up with unfilled 1962 orders. But there was also a healthy demand for this ultimate Corvair, especially among those MG, Triumph, and Porsche owners who found themselves in need of a car with room for a family. The Spyder's "good press" tended to bring a lot of prospective buyers into the showrooms, though many left with just the plain-vanilla Monza. The Spyder remained a specialist machine that, like many of the great ones, was not meant for everybody.

Several changes were made to the Spyder for 1963. These included a wilder cam, standard PCV valve, and removal of the throttle-return check valve. Beginning in mid-1963, the engine compartment sheetmetal was finished in gloss black instead of the exterior paint color. Changes shared with other Corvairs that year included fully transistorized radios, self-adjusting brakes, revised front and rear trim, new hubcaps, upholstery alterations, improved door locks, and the use of exhaust valve rotators.

Spyder production was down in 1964, but still above 1962 levels. Prices remained nearly the same (base price was never higher than $2800). The Spyder was now officially listed as a separate series instead of being a Monza model as in 1962-63. Wheel covers were now unique to the Spyder, and carried the image of (what else?) a gold spider.

The year 1964 was the last for the first-generation Corvair, and the cars saw several changes. Alterations peculiar to the Spyders included chrome plating for the air cleaner and a return to the 1962 camshaft profile. Turbo models received a 12-plate oil cooler and a larger-diameter clutch disc. Greater displacement, now 164 cid, was achieved by lengthening the stroke from 2.60 to 2.94 inches. Predictably, torque was up, but horsepower remained at

for example. Connecting rod column width was increased, and piston rings were made of high-strength centrifugal cast iron. The valve train from the 98-bhp Corvair engine was used, but the exhaust valve heads were made of super-alloy "Nomonic 80A" (largely nickel and chrome), an exotic material needed to withstand exhaust valve temperatures that ran 200 degrees higher than normal.

Once the turbocharged engines met durability standards and the technical problems of knock resistance and matched induction-exhaust had been solved, test units were installed and the cars were flogged at the GM proving grounds. Hitting sustained speeds of well over 100 mph, drivers deliberately tried to induce failures by overheating the engines. Though customers were unlikely to drive that fast or that hard, the engineers would not gamble. Production models were therefore equipped with a temperature gauge "thermister" in the left-hand cylinder head, plus a snap switch at the number-one combustion chamber hooked to a warning light and buzzer. Spyders also had an eight-plate oil cooler (three-plate units were standard).

The result of all this was self-evident: 150 brake horsepower at 4400 rpm, or 1.03 horsepower per cubic inch—over 50 percent more power than the Corvair's 98-bhp engine. Torque shot up 64 percent to 210 foot-pounds at 3200-3400 rpm. Usable power was "up 90 percent," according to Chevrolet; this was at least partly true up to 3400 rpm, but torque fell off rapidly above that.

The Spyder was shown publicly in February 1962, though volume production didn't start until April. The Spyder package was listed as RPO 690, priced at $317.45—quite reasonable considering the extra performance it offered. Orders predictably outstripped capacity. Out of some 152,000 Monza coupes built for 1962, only 6894 emerged as Spyders. There were only 2574 Spyder convertibles out of a total of about 17,000 Monza ragtops. Corvair convert-

150. Both the three- and four-speed transmissions were revised slightly. While the three-speed was theoretically standard on Spyders, few if any were so equipped. The four-speed, now with closer ratios and heavier synchros, was usually ordered.

Probably the most interesting option that year was a set of genuine 13-inch wire wheels supplied by Kelsey-Hayes, complete with special adaptors, nuts, and even a rubber hammer for the "knock-off" hubs. These wheels are extremely rare today as only about 400 or 500 Corvairs were so equipped from the factory. Fewer still, of course, were bolted onto Spyders. Kelsey-Hayes had originally planned to market the wheels separately, but sold its entire production to Chevrolet in 1962. They were officially available during 1963 and 1964 at a price of $403.50, and can bring much more on today's collector market.

Distinguishing among the 1962, '63, and '64 Corvairs is quite easy from the front. The '62s used twin horizontal black "grilles" with horizontal windsplits. The '63s had a full-width horizontal strip with black insert between the headlamps. The 1964 models retained the black insert strip, but added a central emblem in the form of an inverted triangle. Monza Spyder production for model year 1963 amounted to 11,627 coupes and 7472 convertibles. For 1964, the figures were 6480 coupes and 4761 convertibles.

The sleek 1965 Corvair was a design revolution. Good-looking, even from normally unflattering angles, it was a tribute to the fine edge being honed on all GM cars in those days by styling chief William L. Mitchell and his staff. If anything, it looked like the work of an Italian coachbuilder. (In fact, Pininfarina had built a specially-bodied Corvair with similar lines about a year earlier.) Perfectly shaped and never overstated, the second-generation Corvair was one of the great styling achievements of the decade.

For 1965-66, the Monza Spyder gave way as the ultimate Corvair to the 180-bhp turbo-supercharged Corsa. Like the Spyder, the Corsa came in hardtop ($2500) and convertible ($2700) form. In addition to the turbocharged engine, either model was available with a 140-bhp four-carb engine without blower. All Corsas had full instrumentation as standard. Production was 20,291 coupes and 8353 convertibles for the 1965 model year; 7330 coupes and 3142 convertibles for 1966. Of these, 7206 had the turbocharger in '65, and 1951 were so fitted in '66.

But the Corsa was dropped for 1967, partly because of a general tapering off in Corvair development work, and partly because it didn't sell well. The Ford Mustang, its chief competition, could better its performance, and Chevy had its own ponycar for '67 in the Camaro.

Nevertheless, the Corsa was certainly the most advanced production Corvair of all. In turbocharged form, it was more powerful than the Spyder, yet the Corsa coupe weighed about the same as the Spyder coupe. A typical 0–60 mph acceleration time for the turbocharged version was 9.5 seconds; the non-turbo car took 11 seconds. Corsas could hit 115 mph when given enough room, and could average better than 20 miles per gallon when driven at moderate, steady speeds on the highway.

Corvair performance improvements for 1965 reflected further refinements to the flat six. The first Corvair engines had been relatively unstressed, having small ports and valves. For 1965, Chevrolet introduced new cylinder heads similar in shape to the earlier design, but with much larger valves and ports. Intake valve diameter was increased from 1.34 to 1.72 inches; exhaust valves were enlarged from 1.25 to 1.36 inches. The Corsa's turbocharged engine used the same head and cam design as the Monza

Corsa replaced Monza Spyder in the '65 Corvair lineup, featured handsome new shape and hotter turbo engine.

Corsa (1966 coupe shown) lasted only two years. Four-carb engine was standard, turbo optional.

Spyder, but the turbocharger was given wider impeller blades for increased air flow and pressure output, more nozzle area, and more torque.

A total of 80,000 Monza Spyders and Corsas were built over five years. And the cars were interesting enough to attract the attention of those who made it their business to make fast cars faster. A variety of aftermarket accessories thus appeared, some of which were quite successful. Dick Griffin, famous for his Corvair dragsters, developed a special aluminum manifold that allowed the use of a Stromberg WW carburetor. For those who wanted aluminum-bronze valve guides, EMPI could oblige even if Chevy wouldn't. Most modern Corvair enthusiasts wouldn't "wrap" an exhaust system for money, but this was a popular performance tweak in the 1960s. It increased exhaust temperatures, making the gases move faster for higher turbine speeds—at the expense of long life for the crossover pipes. Another non-stock means of boosting horsepower, water injection (seen in production on the Oldsmobile F-85 Jetfire), was also available on the aftermarket. Usually sold in kit form, it included water tanks (often made from aluminum beer kegs) to be mounted in the engine compartment. For $150, Spyders could be equipped with Bill Thomas' "SS" setup consisting of two carburetors and a larger induction tube. With this, the existing turbo pressurized through the carbs instead of drawing its mixture from the stock Carter unit, and was claimed to unleash 40 extra horses.

We've probably seen the end of modified Corvairs. By the late '70s, it was very difficult to find good original Spyders and Corsas, which now command the highest values among all Corvair models. Yet, apart from rebuilding the blower (really a lot easier than it looks), the turbo 'Vairs aren't expensive or difficult to restore. Collectors have tried to preserve as many as possible, but their efforts have been hampered by continuing scrappage. And, of course, some were turned into dune buggies over the years, depleting the ranks of survivors even further.

Nowadays, Monza Spyders and Corsas, both blown and unblown, are again coming to be regarded as the fine automobiles they were. Despite Chevrolet's lackluster support for the Corvair in the face of many ill-bred rumors, these two models actually provided a technological preview of the 1980s. Turbocharging is becoming increasingly common as engineers attempt to resolve the conflict between maintaining performance levels and meeting tighter emissions and fuel economy mandates. It may well be the wave of the future. In the meantime, today's turbocharged cars owe a debt to the Corvair—it was the first.

Though full-size cars remained the most popular in the '60s, Chevrolet had at least shown it was willing to design a small, efficient machine for the enthusiast driver. Yet the irony of the Corvair is that it met an untimely end at the hands of those who claimed to favor sensible cars—almost on the eve of the energy crisis. So, the Corvair was not merely an advanced design—it was a practical one that was ahead of its time.

1966 Corvair Corsa convertible

Camaro 1967-69: Options Were the Story

Just four months after the Mustang hit the streets, it was obvious to GM that Dearborn's quarter-horse was a sales sensation. Accordingly, the Camaro project got the "go" sign from management in August 1964. William L. Mitchell, then design vice-president, calls the first-generation 1967–69 Camaro a "committee design," and partly it was. For economic reasons, certain specifications were laid down that would be practical for the Camaro's "twin under-the-skin," the compact 1968 Chevy II. But the Camaro came first and received the major styling and engineering emphasis.

GM's design theme of that era was termed "fluid." The theory was that if you take a heavy wire frame and bind it into the basic three-dimensional outline of the car you want, then stretch thin canvas over the frame, and finally blow compressed air gently up into the bottom of the canvas envelope, you get a very natural, free-flowing, unartificial body shape. This fluid form showed up in GM's 1965 cars, notably the Corvair, and continued as a corporate look for a number of years afterwards.

Said Henry Haga, whose studio was in charge of Camaro styling: "We felt very strongly about reduc-

ing design to its simplest form, using only one peak down each body side, interrupted by accented wheel arches. The profile of the car also was very simple, using the classic approach of crowned fender lines, with their high points directly above the accented wheel arches ... The canvas-stretched-over-wire theme served to give the Camaro its own character and separated it from the Mustang approach, which was much stiffer and more angular."

So the Camaro had a good-looking shape, with the essential long-hood/short-deck configuration of Ford's ponycar. But more than looks played a part in the success of the Camaro. Like the Mustang, it was really three cars in one: economy, sporty, or high-performance. Through creative use of an extensive option book, the customer could tailor his car to be any of these, or one of an infinite number of variations in between. Marketeers call this the "building-block concept" of packaging.

Camaro prices began at $2466 for the base six-cylinder coupe. The lowest-priced convertible (the only other body style offered) cost $2704. For $26 you could add a larger six, and $106 gave you the base 327 V-8 with 210 horsepower. At this point, you could

Your personalized 1967 Camaro started with the base model in coupe (shown) or convertible form.

1967 Camaro SS-350 sport coupe

contemplate the Rally Sport package, various V-8s offering more power, and the bumblebee-striped Super Sport option.

The Super Sport package initially came only with a 350-cid V-8—an engine exclusive to and introduced with Camaro for 1967. In November 1966, the 396 V-8 was announced in 325-bhp form, and at the same time, Turbo Hydra-Matic became available, but only with the 396.

The 350 and 396 V-8s really deserved the SS package, which included heavy-duty suspension, bumblebee hood stripe, Firestone Wide-Oval tires on six-inch rims, raised hood with finned "oil cooler" inserts, underhood insulation, and SS identification. The SS-396 cost $395, nearly $200 more than the SS-350. (Later the package was offered on its own, regardless of engine.)

The wealth of RPO choices left many a Camaro buyer boggled. But as the essence of this car was in the option book, let's see if we can make some sense of it.

Camaro was offered for '67 in two interior trim

1967 Camaro Super Sport convertible

1967 Camaro Super Sport coupe

New body contours and "peek-a-boo" headlight doors—the 1969 Rally Sport convertible

levels—base and Custom. Carpeting and bucket seats were standard for both, and a front bench seat was also available on either. Additional items in the Custom Interior group included underhood insulation, molded trunk mat, deluxe steering wheel, rear seat armrests with ashtrays, and round courtesy lights in the coupe. Worth noting, too, was a so-called Special Interior group: chromed-plastic windshield pillar moldings, bright-trim pedal pads, and chromed inside roof-rail moldings.

Column-mounted shifters came as standard equipment, but floor shifters were available only if you ordered the central console *and* a four-speed or heavy-duty three-speed manual or the Turbo Hydra-Matic. A special three-dial gauge cluster at $79 was an option for V-8 cars, mounted at the leading edge of the console, which was required. With this gauge pack, the fuel gauge in the right-hand hole on the main dash was replaced by a 7000-rpm tach. Auxiliary instruments comprised combination dials for fuel and engine temperature, oil pressure and amperes, plus a clock.

For the exterior, the next step above the standard Camaro was the Style Trim group: twin-line body pinstriping, anodized aluminum wheel lip moldings, and bright roof gutter moldings. Then came the Rally Sport package for either coupe or convertible at $105 extra. The RS included a special full-width grille with retracting, electrically operated headlight doors; parking lamps in the front valence panel (the standard grille had exposed headlights and grille-mounted parkers); full red taillamps with the backup lights in the valence panel; RS emblems on gas cap, steering wheel hub, front fenders and grille; pinstriping; anodized aluminum rocker moldings; bright wheel lip accents; and chrome drip moldings on coupes.

For wheel dress-up, three optional wheel covers could be ordered separately with all packages. The simulated wires ($74) were popular for the RS, while deep-dish "tulip" covers ($21) were often specified for the SS. There was also a mag-style cover for $74. The five-slot "Rally" wheels were often fitted to the SS and cars with optional disc brakes.

Wheel well speed streaks on '69 Camaro (sport coupe shown) were inspired by Mercedes 300SL

Other noteworthy RPOs included a walnut-grained steering wheel, tilt steering column, headrests, shoulder belts, tinted glass, various radios, tape player, rear speaker, remote outside mirror, electric clock, speed control, vinyl roof, 61-amp alternator, HD radiator, and viscous-drive fan. Power side windows ($100) were also available, though very rare in '67.

Mechanically, the Camaro's standard manual steering had a slow 24:1 ratio. Regular power steering boasted 17.5:1 gearing for 3.0 turns lock-to-lock, and cost only $84. For an additional $16 there was the short-spindle-arm quick-ratio setup that brought manual steering down to an 18:1 ratio, or 15.6:1 with power assist.

Standard brakes were 9.5-inch drums all around, except for 11-inch front drums on the convertible. Sintered metallic linings were optional at $38, and for $79 you could have ventilated front discs with or without vacuum assist ($42). Or you could buy the vacuum booster for any brake setup separately.

One of the best buys for the dollar was the heavy-duty suspension package, which cost only $10.55 and carried RPO numbers F-21 and F-41. This included higher-rate springs and stiffer shocks, and came standard with the Super Sport group and with the 275-bhp 327.

Since the Camaro's curb weight averaged around 3250 pounds, the most potent factory engine allowed was the 325-bhp 396. At the time, GM had an unwritten rule against cars with engines producing more than one horsepower per 10 pounds of vehicle weight. (The 396 Mark IV engine is fully described in Chapter XII.)

The 350-cid V-8 was created by stroking Chevy's 327 from 3.25 to 3.48 inches. Very little else was changed in this engine, which could trace its heritage back to the original 265 of 1955.

At the economy end of the horsepower scale were two sixes, basically identical, and respectable performers. Road tests of the day put fuel economy of the 155-bhp version at 19.1 mpg overall—not bad for a sporty car with a top speed of 107 mph. The 350 V-8's top speed, by the way, was listed by enthusiast magazines at around 120 mph.

On a totally different level, Smokey Yunick prepared two Camaro coupes, a Z-28 and an SS-396, in October 1967, and promptly set 115 class records at Bonneville. The Z-28 topped 174 mph and the 396 did better than 183 mph.

Indianapolis Motor Speedway officials chose Camaro as the pace car for the 1967 500-mile classic. Because of a rainstorm, the race had to be stopped and restarted, so the Camaro paced that year's event twice. In 1969, Camaro was again selected for Indy duty. The '67 pace car was an RS/SS-396 convertible driven by three-time Indy winner Mauri Rose. About 100 pace-car replicas were built, most of them SS-350s with Powerglide. Speedway dignitaries and the motoring press used these cars during race week. Later, they were sold as used cars.

The year 1967 was a good one for Chevrolet, second only to record-breaking 1965 in sales. The Camaro was a big factor. Early demand was so high that dealers sold 46,758 before calendar 1966 had ended, and 220,009 of the '67s altogether. By and large, all ponycars enjoyed a good year, and, as a group, took 13 percent of the American market in '67. The Camaro was joined in its first year by the Mercury Cougar and Pontiac Firebird, while Plymouth gave its Barracuda a new bodyshell and added coupe and convertible styles.

Outwardly, the '68 Camaro looked like nothing had changed, but a lot did: dozens of major and minor alterations. The easiest way to spot a '68 is by its little square side marker lights on each fender—required by federal law that year, and absent on the '67s. Another giveaway is the lack of vent wings on the '68s. Also, the grille came to more of a prow than in '67, with rectangular instead of round parking lamps, and a silver instead of black-painted mesh. The '68 taillamps had vertical splits down each bezel, with the RS using four red lenses and non-RS cars incorporating the white backup lens in the same pod.

The RS, SS, and Style Trim groups were carried over pretty much intact. The RS no longer had standard pinstriping, which could be ordered separately and was relocated from its '67 position. New emblems and thinner rocker moldings with black paint underneath were also RS features for '68. The SS-396 had a black trunk panel (except on black cars) and a hood with 8-blip simulated air intakes. The SS-350 hood kept the fluted "oil cooler" inserts from '67. All SS models now had finned front brake drums as standard equipment. Front discs remained optional, and four-wheel discs became a service option late in the model year for the racing Z-28 only. An all-disc system became a production option for 1969, but only 200 sets were sold.

The big news inside the '68 Camaro was Astro-Ventilation, heralded by little decals on each ventless front window. This flow-through system used swiveling ball nozzles at either end of the instrument panel. These teamed with the regular kick-panel vents to cool driver and passengers top to bottom. You could drive with the windows rolled up because air entered through the cowl and exited via hidden vents in the door jambs.

Most interior equipment and options remained the same as or similar to those in 1967, but the '68 console ($51) wasn't anything like its previous self. Now made entirely of plastic, it was perched atop the tunnel and had little walls on each side to keep things from sliding off. The console gauge cluster ($95) was different too: four rectangular dials arranged in pods of two, one set staggered behind the other. With these gauges came the neatly named Tick-Tock Tach, a 7000-rpm tachometer incorporating an electric clock in its center. This went into the right-hand dial on the dash as a companion for the speedometer.

Engines for '68 also remained essentially the same as before, although the small-block V-8 received larger-diameter main bearings for the new season. Aluminum heads were optional for the 396 and yielded 375 bhp with a special four-barrel Holley carb and other high-performance goodies.

A noteworthy but rarely seen 1968 transmission option was Torque-Drive semi-automatic, introduced in February 1968 for six-cylinder engines only. Priced at about $69, Torque-Drive amounted to Powerglide minus self-shifting. The driver manually selected low or high (or reverse) as needed, using the positively notched column shift. VW offered a similar semi-automatic for about $65 more than Chevrolet's, quizzically named the "Automatic Stick-Shift."

Car Life magazine voted the 1968 Camaro Z-28 one of the ten best cars of the year, and NASCAR handed all '68 Camaros its Industrial Award of Excellence. Sales continued to climb, bettering the 1967 tally by about 15,000. One factor in Camaro's growing market strength was its great success in Trans-Am sedan racing, where it took the 1968 championship by beating a lot of Mustangs. Mustang sales, in fact, were sliding a lot faster than Camaro sales were growing.

A lot happened to Camaro in 1969, the third and final year for the first-generation design. For example, four-wheel discs and variable-ratio power steering made the option book, and body-colored Endura soft front bumpers and cold-air ram induction were offered for the SS and Z-28. Two-toning was available for the first time and there were five (instead of two) vinyl roof colors.

Chevrolet discontinued the 327 engine in February 1969, and a new 307 replaced it as the Camaro's standard V-8. The L-65 350 superseded 1968's high-performance 327, giving the 1969 Camaro two 350s

and four 396s in addition to the Z-28's 302, the base 307, and the two sixes.

According to designer Henry Haga, whose Chevy studio had charge of styling both the first- and second-generation Camaros, the wheel lip brows on the '69 were derived from the Mercedes 300SL gullwing coupe—a car that earlier had influenced some design details on the '58 Impala. The 300SL had very pronounced brows above each wheel cutout. For the Camaro, these were toned down, stretched out, and debossed, leaving speed streaks that blended into the bodyside metal.

The standard '69 grille became deeper set and bolder. Taillamps were longer and thinner, segmented in three angled sections, with backup lights integral on standard models. Fourteen new exterior colors and six two-tone combinations were offered; exterior striping came in red, black, and white.

The popular Rally Sport package again included hidden headlamps, but the covers now had glass ribs so that if the doors failed to open, light could still get through. Another standard RS feature in '69 (optional on other Camaros) was a headlamp washer system— twin nozzles that squirted water onto the lenses on command. A budget version of the RS was the Style Trim option, which included just the bright moldings, headlamp bezel moldings, and fender paint stripes. The Super Sport package carried a black-painted back panel below the trunklid and the same hood as in 1968. But this time, these two items came with all SS engines, not just the 396. Engine dress-up, special paint striping, bright moldings, and SS emblems were also included.

A midyear "Pacesetter Value Package" coincided with Camaro's second tour of duty at the Indy 500. This comprised the 350 V-8, power front discs, whitewalls, and wheel covers.

The year 1969 marked the first time Turbo Hydra-

Sensational GT-inspired Camaro bowed in mid-1970. This is the clean-looking Rally Sport version.

Convertibles were dropped for the second-generation 1970 Camaro. Styling won wide acclaim, would continue into the '80s.

Matic could be ordered with any Camaro engine, even a six. Actually there were two different transmissions, the M-38 (350) and M-40 (400) units. Torque-Drive was continued, again for six-cylinder cars only.

The year had begun with the 210-bhp 327 as the standard V-8, and quite a few '69s were sold with this engine. But in February Chevrolet replaced it with the 307, as mentioned. The four-barrel 327 had already been replaced by the new 350, which in time would become Camaro's base V-8. The 350 took on four-bolt mains, and all 1969 small-blocks included thicker bulkheads and main-bearing caps. They were considerably stronger than the already-strong 1968 blocks.

Two types of ram-air induction systems were offered for '69. One used a special hood with rear-facing inlet. A cold-air duct under the hood mated to the air cleaner via soft rubber gaskets for either single- or twin-carb installations. The other system, carried over from 1967–68, was the dealer-installed cowl plenum ram-air kit, which came with a special air cleaner and adapter for the firewall plenum chamber.

Camaro racked up another SCCA Trans-Am championship in '69, its second in a row. It also was NASCAR's official pace car for eight major stock car races. And it won *Car & Driver* magazine's 1969 readers' poll as the best sporty car. Chevy sold more Camaros than ever.

One reason for the high sales was that the '69 model was sold through early 1970. In February, it was replaced by the second-generation body style. So, many '69s were registered as '70s. Total '69 production was 243,095, but unofficial figures have 53,526 of these listed as "1970" units. These were exactly like the '69s, but their serial numbers contained a zero as the sixth digit. If your car's number reads, say, 124379 it's a genuine '69; number 124370 would be a "1970," or as some call it, a "1969½."

A limited run of 50 Camaros with an *aluminum block* 427 V-8 was made in 1969 "for very special customers." These cars carried a suggested list price of nearly $8600, and were primarily intended for drag racing. Horsepower was nominally rated at 425, but was really much higher, and the car qualified for the NHRA's A/Stock and A/Stock Automatic classes. Executives as well as racers loved it. The story goes that some Chevy managers would take a couple of them out on Woodward Avenue during lunch breaks and dust off everything in sight.

The second-generation Camaro was immediately acclaimed as one of Detroit's most perfectly designed cars. But today, and probably for the near future, collector interest is still centered on the 1967–69s. You can buy one for remarkably little money, and the wide range of options offered means you can probably find the exact car that suits you if you shop around long enough.

Of course if you're a good enough (or brave enough) driver, there is one Camaro in particular to look out for. This one is destined to be the most collectible of the breed, for it has long since become an automotive legend. Its name: Z-28.

1970 Camaro sport coupe

Camaro Z-28: The Living Legend

You can still buy a Camaro Z-28 today, thanks to the enthusiasm of a lot of people at Chevrolet Division. The more recent versions, however, are considerably different from the first Zs of 1967–70.

Vincent W. Piggins, who started as a Chevy engineer in 1956, deserves much of the credit for the original Z-28. "After Ford released the Mustang," Piggins said, "they had about two years on us before Chevrolet could get the Camaro into the 1967 product line. I felt in my activity, which deals with product promotion and how to get the most promotional mileage from a car from the performance standpoint, that we needed to develop a performance image for the Camaro that would be superior to the Mustang's.

"Along comes SCCA in creating the Trans-Am sedan racing class for professional drivers in 1966, aimed for the 1967 season . . . I suggested a vehicle that would fit this class and . . . it gave them the heart to push ahead and make up the rules, regulations, and so forth for the Trans-Am series. I feel this was really the creation of the Trans-Am as we know it."

What qualified the Camaro as a "sedan" was the fact that it had rear seats. Although Chevrolet sold only 602 Z-28s during 1967, they met the 1000-car minimum-production rule by homologating the 350-cid Camaro under FIA Group I rules, and then qualifying the same basic vehicle with the Z-28 option under Group II.

Piggins originally proposed using the 283 V-8 and F-41 heavy-duty suspension for the Z-28, along with front disc brakes and metallic-lined rear drums, close-ratio four-speed, new 24:1-ratio steering gear, Corvette 15×6 wheels with 7.75 tires, and a reworked hood with a functional air intake. He received permission to have a prototype built to these initial specs, and introduced it to top management at the proving grounds in October 1966. Division general manager Elliott M. "Pete" Estes (now GM president) tried the prototype and liked it.

Continued Piggins: "While we were driving the car, I mentioned that we'd put the 283 into it because we'd built that size engine before. But I suggested . . . that it might be a lot better to take the 327 block and put the 283 crank into it, giving us a 4×3 bore and stroke. That would put displacement at 302.4 cid, just under the SCCA's 305 limit. So Pete immediately agreed, especially being an engineer and knowing the potential this car could have."

Chevrolet built up a prototype 302-engined show car, and displayed it to the press at a special preview at Riverside Raceway in California. The equipment was labeled as Regular Production Option (RPO) Z-28. All the writers and editors who drove this first Z-28 loved it, and published rave reviews afterward. There is no truth to the rumor that the "Z" in Z-28 stood for Zora Arkus-Duntov, the great Corvette engineer. It just followed the RPO numerical sequence after Z-27, the early Camaro Super Sport package. "The graphics people did things with the

Z-28 could be combined with other option groups as in this 1968 RS coupe.

MICHAEL LAMM

1971 Camaro Z-28

Z, and that's how the designation stuck," said Piggins.

Camaro Z-28s won the Trans-Am championship two years running, 1968 and 1969. The resulting publicity helped Camaro sales immeasurably. Not that the Z-28 you could buy over the counter in those years was anything like the cars that won in SCCA competition. Roger Penske, Mark Donohue, Smokey Yunick, Ronny Bucknum, Jerry Thompson, Tony De-Lorenzo, and other professionals ran Z-28s honed to an incredibly fine edge. But as people like Penske and Donohue learned more about what they needed to win races, Chevrolet began making and cataloguing the necessary parts. These were immediately available to everyone.

Specifications for the 1967–69 production Z-28s list horsepower as 290 at 5800. But it's important to keep in mind that this was a nominal figure—somebody just plugged it into the spec sheets. It might as well have been 300 or 350 or 500 bhp. Most, if not all, 302 Z-28s put out more than 290 bhp and 290 foot-pounds of torque at 4200 rpm.

Actual horsepower depended on which intake and exhaust manifolds you chose, which carburetor(s),

and what internal mods you made. No actual dyno figures were ever released for the 302, but magazine estimates ran from a realistic 350 bhp by *Road & Track* to 400 bhp by *Car Life*. All-out, blueprinted racing versions, like those built by Traco and Yunick, probably delivered around 450 bhp, which took some heavy tinkering to pull from 302 cubes without compromising reliability. Whatever the "street" Zs had, Chevy didn't flinch and they carried the same 2-year/24,000-mile overall warranty and 5-year/50,000-mile powertrain warranty as other Chevrolets.

The first 25 Z-28s were built between December 29, 1966 and January 12, 1967, and went to favored dealers, mostly for reworking as competition cars. But it wasn't long before enthusiastic potential customers were pounding on the salesroom doors. If you'd been interested in a Z-28 in, say, 1968, you'd be faced with a rather lengthy procedure. First, order a conventional Camaro six-cylinder coupe at a $2964 base price. Add to that the Z-28 equipment—the 302 V-8, F-41 HD suspension, Corvette Rally wheels and Goodyear Wide Tread GT tires, Z-28 paint striping on hood and deck, N-44 quick steering (non-power) option, and 302 front-fender emblems. Along with the $400 Z-28 package, you also had to order two "mandatory options": front disc brakes with vacuum assist at $100, and one of three available four-speed transmissions ($184 minimum). So right away you started with an equipment group that added nearly $700 to the price of a basic Camaro coupe. (The Z-28 was never offered as a convertible.)

You might want to toss in additional goodies like the RS package ($105), the tack-on fiberglass rear spoiler ($33), Positraction ($42), the still-quicker N-40 power steering ($84), and the sintered metallic rear linings ($38). A set of fabricated steel-tube headers came from the factory for about $200 extra, but were simply left in the trunk and had to be dealer-installed. The twin four-barrel manifold with dual Holley 600-cfm carbs added another $500 or so, and also

MICHAEL LAMM

1968 Camaro Z-28 sport coupe (with RS option)

had to be dealer-installed. Finally, the cowl-plenum ram-air system came to $79. So a fully-optioned Z-28 could easily exceed $5000. (How times and dollar values change!)

For the 1970 season, SCCA rules were rewritten to allow destroking for the first time. This was done mainly to allow Chrysler, which had only the 273 and 318 V-8s, to compete with AMC, GM, and Ford. Under the new rules, there was no need for Chevy to hang onto the 302, because the 350 could be downsized exactly the same way the 327 had been. The 350 had the same bore as the 327, so the crankshaft from the 283 V-8 fit just as before.

Thus, in the interest of deproliferation, the 350 became the Z-28's new engine for "1970½," coinciding with the appearance of the exquisitely styled second-generation Camaro from the studio of Henry Haga. Chevrolet rated the Camaro 350 at 10 bhp less than the corresponding LT-1 Corvette engine. Torque, though, was the same in both: 380 foot-pounds.

According to many writers, engineers, and owners, the 1970½ Z-28, with its new engine and new body style, beat the socks off any Z-28 before it—and all of those that followed. The LT-1 proved more tractable, more reliable, had more torque off the line, and generally outperformed the more highly stressed 302 in every way. It was also the first Z-28 with stock front disc brakes, front and rear anti-roll bars, a new front suspension that gave less understeer, and more comfortable seats, plus a much better insulated and quieter body. Turbo Hydra-Matic became a Z-28 option for the first time, and there was little difference in performance between it and the four-speed manual.

Vince Piggins stated that a steel, cold-air-ducted hood was available for 1970½ and that Chevrolet had earlier tried a Corvette-type scoop hood for that year. But John DeLorean, Chevrolet's new general manager, didn't like that hood, calling it a "coffin." Also, SCCA rules for 1970 didn't allow a raised hood de-

sign. "So we built an internal cold-air hood—an internally ducted design that picked up cold air ahead of the radiator," Piggins said. "That was the first time we ever used that innovation in the Camaro."

The 1970½ Z-28 shared its overall body configuration with tamer Camaros, but several distinctions set it apart. Wide stripes on the hood and deck made the Z stand out as before, as did two different deck spoilers offered that year. Standard in 1970½ and 1971 was a low-profile one-piece spoiler, very much like that of 1967–69, bolted to the decklid and overlapping the rear fenders slightly on each side. Then in April 1970, an entirely different, optional spoiler arrived—the same tall, three-piece ducktail that's still used today. "We needed a bigger spoiler for the new Z-28," Piggins said, "but new tooling would have been quite expensive, with a lead time of at least six months. So we borrowed the Firebird's center section . . . Camaro designers did individualize the end caps, but the center section was and is strictly Firebird."

The only Chevrolet engines to escape a 1971 GM-wide edict of 8.5:1 maximum compression (allowing the use of unleaded gas) were the Z-28 and a few Corvettes, all of which ended up with 9.0:1 compression through 1974. But for 1972 the Z-28's horsepower rating slid to 255 net, then to 245 in 1973–74. Solid lifters gave way to a hydraulic cam for 1973, though the same high engine quality persisted: four-bolt mains, baffled pan, big-valve heads, etc. And for 1973, due to the addition of exhaust gas recirculation (EGR), the high-rise aluminum intake manifold succumbed to a conventional cast-iron version that mounted a Rochester Quadrajet carburetor instead of the previous high-performance Holley. It marked the end of an era.

Beginning in 1972, there was an optional spoiler package that included a front air dam, and variable-ratio power steering gave way to a straight power system with a 16:1 ratio. The good, all-foam Camaro

Optional front air dam and new cold-air hood set the 1969 Z-28 apart from other Camaros.

seats introduced in 1970½ had been replaced by modified Vega perches during 1971. For 1973, the price of the Z-28 option dropped abruptly, from a high of $786.75 in 1971 to $502.05. Camaros were still selling briskly, though a nearly fatal 174-day United Auto Works Union strike at the Norwood, Ohio F-body assembly plant all but ended the Camaro's life.

The '74 model featured the aluminum bumpers, revised nose and grille, and wraparound taillamps as on other Camaros. The Z-28 specifically received big lettering on hood and deck. With the Arab oil embargo of December 1973, rising insurance rates for high-performance cars, and increasing government regulations, GM dropped the Z-28 rather than water it down more.

Zs continued to race, and it's logical to assume that the good publicity contributed to its return in February 1977. But instead of a simple decal package or a muscle car, Chevy brought it back as a "handler." The new package was much more of a suspension and steering option than one intended for brute strength.

For this reborn Z-car, Chevy made the front and rear springs tauter, increased diameter of the front anti-roll bar, and put on larger wheels and tires. Front spring rates went from 300 pounds per inch in 1974 to 365 for 1977–78. Rear rates rose to 127 pounds per inch from 89–99. The previous 1-inch front stabilizer was replaced by a 1.2-inch bar, and its rear mate was slimmed to 0.55-inch from 1974's 0.6875-inch. Front shock valving stayed the same (identical with that of the optional F-41 suspension), but the rear was slightly revised to match the thinner anti-roll bar. Said engineer Jack Turner, Jr., who worked on these suspension changes: "We decided to make a road machine out of the Z-28, and not a dragster. Emissions and fuel requirements restricted what could be done to the engine, so we concentrated on handling. We wanted to make the vehicle feel that it was positively with you all the time—that the steering wheel was glued to the road without a rubber band in between.

"We tried to pick a happy medium between going up in spring rates and still not having to add humungous stabilizer bars. We tried to balance the system so the car could go over road undulations and go into corners with chatter bumps so that the suspension would allow the tires to envelop some of that roughness instead of skidding across the tops. That means a lot of refinement between the shock valving, spring rate, and stabilizer bar rate. You've got to balance the whole package together."

Turner's people also speeded up the steering ratio from the previous overall 14.3:1 to 13.02:1. Power assist was still standard, but the variable-ratio feature was eliminated. Quite a bit of time was spent in tire selection. The final choice was a steel-belted GR70-15, which also turned out to be the Corvette tire. These were mounted on new 15×7-inch Z-28 wheels.

1970 Camaro Z-28 sport coupe

Horsepower for the 1977½ Z-28 came in at 185 bhp net, with 280 foot-pounds of torque—low but ample. Gone were the four-bolt mains, the forged crank, and any vestige of a long-duration cam.

The Z-28's four-speed was now a Borg-Warner T-10 with a nicely refined shifter. Turbo Hydra-Matic became mandatory in California and much favored elsewhere. Axle ratios were chosen to complement the car's cornering ability. "We got the vehicle very responsive and very close to neutral when you apply power," continued Jack Turner. "If you go around a corner under power, you end up with a nice neutral drift—or you can even trick it into an oversteer if you want to."

Not only did the revived Z-28 now handle in the best GT tradition, it also looked good. The 1977 graphics impressed everyone—the blacked-out paint, highlighted with decal-trimmed wheel lip moldings and bold Z-28 signs front and rear, contrasted beautifully with the tricolor taillamp ensemble. It was a striking car from any angle. Spoiler and air dam were now standard, and buyers had a choice of colors and comfort options.

"We were interested in putting together a quality, handling, durable machine. Throughout the whole program, cost wasn't the object, as long as we had the pieces available," concluded Turner. And the pieces fit together remarkably well.

The basic Z-28 package continued for 1978, but in 1979 the engine lost 10 net bhp. The 1980 edition still came standard with the top-of-the-line 350-cid V-8 but was less powerful. For 1981, the Z-car will offer computer-controlled carburetion for both engines (standard 305-cid V8 and optional 350 V-8) and a lock-up torque converter clutch (effective on both second and third gears) on automatic-equipped cars for greater fuel economy.

Camaros of the '80s will undoubtedly change (the 1982 edition will have an all-new bodyshell and major mechanical revisions). With Detroit now beginning to get a handle on lively, efficient cars, we can probably look for more good cars wearing the Z-28 label in the future. One thing's for sure: every one of them since 1967 has been something special, and today's Z-28 owners are a lucky lot indeed.

For the Enthusiast: Great Books on Chevrolet

The Great Camaro, by Michael Lamm, 11×8.75 inches, 144 pages, 287 photos, 21 in color, $14.95. Published by Lamm-Morada Publishing Company, Box 7207, Stockton, CA 95207.

Former *Special-Interest Autos* editor Michael Lamm is author of this jam-packed Camaro history, filled with photographs and a readable text. In particular, the book depicts renderings, clays, and running prototypes of Camaros born and unborn, and is filled with firsthand accounts by designers, engineers, and executives. This is really the definitive Camaro history, and it deserves the good reception it has received since its release in 1978.

The layout of the book is horizontal, with somewhat small, though clean, type and well-edited text. The nine chapters vary in length from two pages ("The Camaro Debut") to 42 pages ("First Generation Camaros"). Two extensive sections discuss the ultimate racing machine, the Z-28, and the Camaro's impressive racing record. Print quality is excellent, with clear black-and-white pictures and good reproduction in the color section. Heavy coated pages are wrapped in tough covers and tightly sewn together, so the book is not likely to fall apart. Lamm's work is priced right, especially for such a detailed car book in these inflationary times.

The Hot One: Chevrolet 1955–1957, by Pat Chappell, 11×8.5 inches, 208 pages, 250 illustrations, 10 in color, $21.95. Published by Dragonwyck Publishing Inc., Box 385-G, Contoocook, NH 03229.

At this writing, *The Hot One* is in its second edition and fourth printing, and has received a uniformly high rating from reviewers and Chevy enthusiasts alike. Its subject, of course, is the significant 1955–1957 period. Based on five years of research, the book includes numerous interviews with the designers and engineers who shaped Chevrolet's history after World War II. There are six lengthy chapters—one for each of the three model years, one for the Nomad alone, an introductory chapter on Chevrolet's postwar development, and a follow-up entry on what happened in 1958 and later. A large appendix includes production figures, specifications, color combinations, accessories, and prices.

For the second edition (according to the publisher, only a dozen alterations were necessary) *The Hot One* was issued with a special silver binding, and a logo honoring the 25th anniversary of the 1955 Chevrolet. The quality of illustrations is excellent and the text is ample and well-edited.

Sixty Years of Chevrolet, by George H. Dammann, 8.75×11 inches, 320 pages, 1550 illustrations, all black-and-white, $18.95. Published by Crestline Publishing, 1251 N. Jefferson Ave., Sarasota, FL 33577.

This was the third book in the Crestline marque series, following similar works by the same author on Ford and Lincoln-Mercury. One of the highest-selling books of its type, it remains the only complete book on Chevrolet. The Crestline formula is pictorial, as virtually every page is devoted mostly to photographs of production models, with individual captions usually detailing original list price, number produced, and other data.

The great strength of the Crestline books is in their reference value. The reader can rapidly locate almost any Chevrolet model and body style ever made by turning to the appropriate chapter—there's one for each model year from "pre-Chevrolet" 1912 onward. The book's disadvantage is its lack of historical perspective—the whys and wherefores of Chevy's moves. There is also very little on competition history. However, the photographs are of good quality, and the book well-bound in heavy-duty vinyl.

Corvette: America's Only True Sports Car, by the Editors of Consumer Guide®, 8.5×11.5 inches, 96 pages, 150 illustrations, 21 in color, $5.95. Available from Dragonwyck Publishing, Inc., Box 385-G, Contoocook, NH 03229.

The hardbound version of *Consumer Guide's*® Corvette history provides a detailed chronicle of America's only surviving sports car, including anecdotes about the people responsible for its development, and colorful photographs from every period of its evolution.

The book begins with a view of the American sports car movement after World War II, then goes on to the factors that led to the first Corvette of 1953. Two people instrumental in the car's design over the years, engineer Zora Arkus-Duntov and stylist Bill Mitchell, are interviewed individually. The 'Vette's accomplishments on the race track are recalled, and there's a section devoted to the famous 1978 Corvette Indy Pace Car and pace car replicas. Corvette show cars, among the most dramatically styled machines of their day, are also given special attention. Corvette enthusiasts will find this a valuable addition to their library, but anyone who likes cars will enjoy this popularly priced book on one of Chevy's most imaginative automobiles.